F
RELATIONS

"Jaya Sila and Vimala's 5 Drop Rescue Remedy is the most concise practical Krishna conscious guide on developing good relationships that I have seen. It is both down to earth and Sastra based."

– MAHATMA DASA,
ISKCON INITIATING GURU

"I really love Jaya Sila and Vimala's focus on developing relationships around success. The approach is so effective that it brings one quickly back onto the positive path."

–ANANDA VRNDAVANA DEVI DASI,
TEMPLE PRESIDENT, WASHINGTON DC

The Relationship Rescue Remedy course is extremely important. I am looking forward to have this course introduced as a basis before one enters into Krishna Consciousness with advanced Vaishnava philosophy. Without accepting relationships there is a danger to get 'sophisticated animalism', using high philosophy and denying the needs etc. of sincere devotees. I am extremely thankful to Jaya Sila and Vimala Prabhus for having started this course. I wish them to come to Radhadesh and give seminars about it. We coming together every week here and go through this course. Your servant, Ramananda Raya Dasa.

– RAMANANDA RAYA DASA,
ISKCON RADHADESH, BELGIUM

Acyuta dd and I would like to express our gratitude for the valuable relationship tools you have provided us. The five drop exercises are complementary tools to assist couples, more specifically grihasthas in the rigors of relationship management. We, both being professional counselors, are sometimes more burdened with what we think we know works and what doesn't. Yet in this case, we were enthusiastic to model these exercises because of its saturation in Vedic principles. In summation, dropping the flame, blame, vain, pain and pouring it on (affirmation) is a brilliant tool to derive loving relationships that extend past couples. I envision the value of these drops if only others I have had relationship issues with could participate.

– ACYUTA DASI AND CANDRA DAS
PROFESSIONAL COUNSELLORS

FACEBOOK FEEDBACK

 Bhakti Rasa My name is Bhakti, I am feeling very grateful that this course has been created and is now available to the worldwide ISKCON community. I am not sure how I came in contact with this course but already after only watching three episodes of RRR, I am experiencing a shift in my outlook and perception of past present and future personal interactions. I have read dozens of self development and relationship guidance books, but what I have learned from your course in some way has been more effective! Sending blessing and prayers to the remarkable service of Jay Sila das and his wonderful wife and all others who have been involved in this pioneering endeavour.

Unlike · Reply · 🔘 4 · March 20, 2016 at 8:05pm

 Vimala Howie Thanks for sharing that. We are so glad you getting some benefit and that it is all making sense to you!

Unlike · Reply · 🔘 4 · March 22, 2016 at 5:17am

 Bhakti Rasa Getting some benefit is an understatement! I am getting heaps of benefit. Both you and your husband have succeeded in conveying with clarity the essence of what one needs to do or avoid. The formula is easy to understand and simple to practice.

Unlike · Reply · 🔘 1 · March 22, 2016 at 8:01am

– BHAKTI RASA DASA, ISKCON 2ND GENERATION

 Krishna Bhavana
April 11, 2016

Hare Krsna Jay SilaPrabhu and Vimala Mataji, plpleaze accept my humble obeiances. All glories to Srila Prabhupada. All glories to your wonderful service to the devotees which is fundamentally very important to take our relrelationships to a higher level.

There are so many other courses, seminars, counselling are there to help with communication and relationship. The wonderful fact here is that you are quoting Srila Prabhupada and His Books which is amazingly and beautiful. So clearly explained. So easy to understand. And we getting the priviledge of your association. I pray I will acquire everything that your course is making available to us. Thank you so much. Your servant

🔘🔘 You, Vimala Howle, Caitanya Carana Dasa and 4 others   3 Comments

🔘 Love   💬 Comment

– KRISHNA BHAVANA, BRISBANE, AUSTRALIA

Relationship
Rescue Remedy
(Devotee Edition)

*The Five Drop Formula
for Restoring and Maintaining
Healthy Relationships*

Jaya Sila & Vimala Howie

February 2017

ISBN: 978-1-54321-248-8

DEDICATION

We dedicate this book to our eternal spiritual master, His Divine Grace A.C. Bhaktivedanta Swami Prabhupada, who wanted so much that his disciples and followers learn how to live cooperatively in Krishna Consciousness.

"We require so many householders to set the example for others, how in Krishna consciousness we can live peacefully and sanely, even in married life."

−SRILA PRABHUPADA LETTER TO NANDAKISORA DASA, 11TH DECEMBER 1968

We pray that our humble attempts are pleasing to His Divine Grace.

ACKNOWLEDGEMENTS

We would like to acknowledge one of our dear friends and 'human relationship' mentors, Howard Glasser, the founder of The Nurtured Heart Approach®.

Howard's approach nicely reflects the Vaisnava way of always nurturing the good in others. It's what our Vaisnava Acaryas and specifically Srila Prabhupada termed... becoming like the 'honey bee'. Howard, who loves kirtan and has read Srila Prabhupada's biography, recognizes the 'honey bee' principle as fundamental to the success of all spiritual and interpersonal relationships.

Thanks to Madri Devi Dasi for proof reading and to Krsnendu Dasa and Dina Bandhu Dasa for their technical assistance. Our thanks also goes to all the other people who directly and indirectly helped to complete our book.

We would also like to thank our wonderful and tolerant family for constantly supporting and encouraging us in our endeavours. Our daughter Saraswati, our son Navadvipa Lila, (formerly Nanda-Lal) and his wife Adina Lila have taught us, each in their own unique and special way, how to develop authentic relationships based on love and trust. And last, but not least, we acknowledge our 3-year- old granddaughter, Murali for being a constant source of joy and fun.

TABLE OF CONTENTS

Chapter 3
Drop Three – Drop the Blame (Accept Responsibility) 57

Chapter 4
Drop Four – Drop the Pain (Reconnect with Your Higher Self) . 71

INTRODUCTION:

The Birth of the Relationship Rescue Remedy

It was around 2:30am one winter morning when the Five Drop Rescue Remedy was born. Of course it didn't have the catchy title then. Actually, my husband and I were in the middle of a 'meltdown'. Yes, you heard right. It was a meltdown at 2:30 in the morning! But what was worse, or even darkly funny, was that it happened in the middle of our first session of trying to write a book together about successful Grihastha life. Our embryonic book, entitled, 'The Grihastha Journey' was envisioned as a comprehensive manual, gleaned from 40 years of practical experience. We were determined and enthusiastic to write this book amid our hectic schedules as teachers, thus the 'earlier than early' rising schedule.

So, there we sat, enveloped in tension, with time ticking carelessly away and the two lower modes of nature wreaking their havoc upon us. Our struggle stemmed mainly from our very discordant styles of how to approach the task. My husband's approach to a given task is very logical and linear, while I lean heavily on creativity and spontaneity - raring to go, but finding it hard to tune into the routine minutiae required. We always joke that it is lucky we never had an astrological compatibility chart done or we would have definitely flunked.

You will be relieved to know that we worked to the other side of our conflict, as we always do, and have done for the last 40 years! However, we had just used up our precious writing period and were now feeling the frustration of time wasted. Or was it? It was at this juncture that we realised that the process of how we worked through our conflicts could be a useful formula. We had consistently found when counselling couples, that they either had few, or very ineffective, tools to solve their misunderstandings. We began to see how our experience in effectively solving conflicts could be both valid and useful.

Consequently, on that fateful, chilly morning our enthusiasm was diverted to working out the steps we used to solve all those upsets and conflicts over the years. We quickly discovered that the process had a definite structure; one that had evolved and matured over the years into a formula. At this point, we concluded that a different book was required; one with a focus on urgently needed communication skills, specifically how to solve conflicts. But do not be too concerned. 'The Grihastha Journey' with its many started, but incomplete chapters awaits us patiently, suspended somewhere in Microsoft Word. It has readily taken a backseat to what we consider both urgent and important; 'Relationship Rescue Remedy', a time-tested, uncomplicated recipe that will help you to easily dissolve conflicts.

These conflicts, both big and small, are the ones that eat away at the very fibre of our most cherished relationships. We have observed the impact of destroyed relationships within our ISKCON society, and the effect this has had on devotees' spiritual and material lives. We have also witnessed the legacy of these consequences spilling over to second and now third generations, the children Srila Prabhupada confidently labelled as our *'future hope'*. But there is no need to get depressed. Acknowledging such serious social implications can and should be a positive motivating force for change. We are confident that using the effective conflict resolution strategies outlined in our Relationship Rescue Remedy can help turn the tide on this disturbing trend.

Why it Matters So Much

Now let me shout this out loudly for everyone to hear- having what you consider to be an Okay relationship with your spouse is **not Okay!** Frankly speaking, if that's our current thinking, chances are the vast majority of us will end up settling for **less** than Okay relationships. Isn't that how everything else in life works? Unless we aim for extraordinary (great) relationships, the reality will be less than satisfactory. As devotees we have made a commitment to work towards becoming great souls. Why should we lessen our expectations in the relationships department?

Unfortunately a large majority of devotees still hold the misconception that the acceptable standard of excellence for our Grihastha ashram is to have an mediocre relationship; translation-to weather the storm for around 25 years and come out the other side, still in one piece. It appears that our societal expectation for successful family life hasn't progressed much from those early, and often dysfunctional days, when the best relationship training programs offered, were 'The Hopes and Horrors of Household Life' or the equally dismal 'Survival in The Grihastha Ashrama'.

In recent years, with the desire to reverse negative trends, we have seen ISKCON leadership making concerted efforts to cultivate and expect high standards of excellence from both the Brahmacari and Sannyasa ashrams. The word is out that excellence is the way to go. But what about the other 95% of ISKCON's membership- our Grihastha ashram? Will aiming for Okay make them happy, will it provide an inspiring example for their children to emulate? I don't think so!

Srila Prabhupada was so embarrassed at the level of immaturity in our marital relationships that he once remarked that he wanted nothing further to do with the marriages of his disciples and that they should marry at their own risk.

"Yes, the two marriages may be performed by you, but only after having sufficiently counseled the respective devotees. This business should not be taken as a farce, but is a very serious matter. Recently so many couples have been sent adrift by the waves of maya's influence. That is hard to check, but still the devotees must realize the responsibilities of household life. And there is no question of separation. Too much this has been happening and I am very much displeased..."

**– SRILA (PRABHUPADA TO BHAGAVAN,
LOS ANGELES, JULY 7, 1971**

Loving Relationship - Sentiment or Essential?

The Grihastha ashram is the foundational building block of Vedic varnashrama society. It is imperative that we acknowledge this fact. Unfortunately the trend is for devotees to minimise the importance of this ashram. Research and history carries the evidence of how important a peaceful family life is to any society. One senior devotee shared with my husband that when he entered into married life he naively intended to give his relationship as little energy as possible, thus saving his time for the more important things in his life such as sadhana and service. Sound familiar? I am sure this will ring a bell with many. This is what happens when we separate our Krishna Consciousness from our relationships. *'Here's my relationship over here...and here is my Krishna Consciousness over there. Of course, I want to be Krishna Conscious, not entangled in household life, so I will give that part as little time and energy as possible.'* This may sound logical to some, but factually it never works like that. In this devotee's own words his starvation strategy nearly 'killed' his marriage.

The first and overriding principle in the husband-wife relationship is the unrelenting desire of both individuals to make their marriage work through Krsna consciousness.

**– VISHAKA DEVI DASI, VAISNAVA FAMILY
& YOUTH CONFERENCE**

Srila Prabhupada envisioned Grihastha couples working co-operatively and peacefully to progress in their spiritual life. As devotees our existence certainly revolves around our sadhana and service, but our relationships form a huge part of this equation. When we work with devotees on any given service or project there is a necessity of developing relationships based on love and trust. To do this we have to 'feed' our relationships with time and energy, as well as learn healthy ways to work out misunderstandings and conflicts. Our marital relationship is no different. To serve together nicely we need to develop and nurture a mood of love and cooperation. Otherwise the very service and sadhana we so earnestly wish to preserve, will ultimately be disrupted on one level or other.

The North American Grihastha Vision team also recognizes the urgency of reversing the current trend and encouraging successful family life.

Let's reflect upon the mood of our founder acharya. Whenever there was a lack of something necessary, Srila Prabhupada prioritized the missing thing. For example, he focused on brahminical development because brahmanas (the heads) were the most absent in our society. He acted in many emergency ways to address this absence. Because the marriage and family situation is in emergency or crisis mode, we should make shoring up marriages and families a priority in ISKCON!

Grihastha devotees everywhere are crying out for guidance that supports and encourages the unique aspects of their ashram. Our online-course and this book which acts as an accompaniment or stand-alone resource, aims at helping to fill that void. It delivers a practical five step method which teaches how to diffuse and resolve conflicts, so that *'living together peacefully'* can become a constant reality and not just a hopeful dream!

Apply Liberally to all Relationships

Although our book is written mainly in the context of marital interactions, it doesn't take much to discern that the tools and strategies we present can be applied successfully in any relationship dynamic. Srila Prabhupada, disturbed by the constant fighting of his fledgling disciples, urged in a letter to Rayarama dasa as early as February 1969.

An old father required massaging so all the children wanted to serve the father. The father divided the right and left portion of his body to be served by the children. Later, along with the service, there was some quarrel between the children and they were competing by hitting the parts of the father that were assigned to the opposing party. The father said that you are hitting my different parts due to your opposition to one another, but I am therefore dying. If there is any misunderstanding, please live peacefully.

Unsettled conflicts also play a sizable role in why we lose precious devotees. It is generally not philosophical doubt, or even the austerities and rigours of spiritual life, that pushes away our numbers; it lies in the culminating effect of years of constant bickering, misunderstandings and unresolved issues that we either *won't*, or possibly *can't*, deal with.

And we are not alone. The *'back door'* is the metaphorical term which describes people leaving various church denominations. The top reasons reported as to why people stop attending their given church, has been cited as 'gossip and unresolved conflict.'

An Important Note

This book is not meant to cover all aspects of marriage and relationships in Krishna Consciousness. We will not go into gender roles, expectations or other issues which are all relevant to Krishna Conscious married life, but which are beyond the scope of this book. Such important topics and much more will be included in our next publication entitled:

The Grihastha Journey. Think of this little book as a practical first aid kit. It will give you five steps or 'drops' that will enable you to quickly clear away any festering conflicts. And, just so you don't have to skim the chapters to see what they are here is a quick overview.

The Five Drops... A Sneak Preview

Drop No. 1 Drop the Flame - (Pause)

As the name implies, this is about learning ways to drop the heat in a burgeoning conflict. It is a powerful and crucial first step which paves the way for entry into rational and genuine communication.

Drop No. 2 Drop the Vain - (Reflect)

This drop is pivotal. Here you will learn how relationships aren't simply about you. You'll learn how to 'reflect' and understand the other person's perspective. It takes two people to be in a 'relationship'. Until you can do this, you will remain stuck in the vicious cycle of attack and defend.

Drop No. 3 Drop the Blame - (Accept Responsibility)

This one is about accepting responsibility for both your part in the upset and for bringing it to a resolution. The principle of accepting responsibility is one that interlaces intrinsically through all the five drops.

Drop No. 4 Drop the Pain - (Realign with your higher self)

Drop Four will teach you how to move beyond all your past issues. It's about getting back to our best state; the place we strive and aspire to be in. You'll then be ready to put your heads together and come up with alternative solutions.

Drop No. 5 Pour on the Energy! - (Take your relationship to the next level)

This last drop is one we all need more of. No need for drops here, we can pour this one on. It's all about focusing on what is going right and re-directing your energy towards it.

In Search of Utopia

Many devotees get discouraged when they encounter conflict in their relationships. *"Hey, it's just not supposed to be like this..."* *"I joined Krishna Consciousness to escape from all this!"* We whinge, we whine and wax on; but it changes nothing.

Although our Utopian ideals sound noble, they can often leave us frustrated and disappointed. They can also result in us becoming negative and impersonal in our dealings. Srila Prabhupada warned about this tendency in a letter to Atreya Rsi dasa in 1972.

So we shall not expect that anywhere there is any Utopia. Rather, that is impersonalism. People should not expect that even in the Krishna Consciousness Society there will be Utopia. Because devotees are persons, therefore there will always be some lacking – but despite everything they may do, their topmost intention is to serve Krishna.

We need to live and work with this reality. Even the most successful marriages have upsets. Many look towards Vaisnava couples whose relationships have passed the test of time and muse naively, *"Oh, they must get on all the time. I bet they never argue."* I don't want to burst any bubbles here, but... I dare you...just go and ask them!

Conflict is not the Real Problem

It's important to remember that avoiding conflict should never be our focus. It's learning how to effectively deal with our misunderstandings and conflicts that is the secret key to successful relationships. There was a time when I also equated conflict with failure. I would carefully avoid conflict using repression, which I successfully masked in a veneer of pseudo tolerance. I got very good at quietly smoothing things over. Eventually this kind of repression culminates in a buildup of resentment, which is never healthy. Over the years I have radically changed my belief in this regard. *If dealt with and resolved properly, conflicts are not only normal and healthy - but they have the power to strengthen us and even bring us closer.*

In our Western paradigm, with diminishing family values and a structure that neglects both respect and etiquette, even slight upsets can quickly escalate into mammoth proportions. When our relationships fall into this emotionally draining 'too hard' basket, our contemporary western solution urges us to jump ship and opt for change. Therefore divorce is rampant.

Fortunately we ***don't*** and ***won't*** have to go there. What you are about to learn in the pages of this short book, will give you a process that will teach you how to deal with any conflict in a sane and rational manner. Once this becomes habitual you will no longer fear becoming one of the frightening divorce statistics. So, let's get started with **Drop One - Drop the Flame**.

CHAPTER 1

Drop the Flame (Pause)

"Something has dropped in the water, in the river. You cannot see the thing dropped within the water by agitating the water. Just stand still for some time. As soon as the water is settled up, you'll see the things as they are. So as soon as our enthusiasm is agitated, it is better to sit down in any temple suitable and chant Hare Krishna. There is no question of being disappointed. After all, we commit so many mistakes. That is human nature. To err is human. That is not fault. But try to rectify with cool head."

– LECTURE - THE NECTAR OF DEVOTION - CALCUTTA, 27-1-73

Drop the flame simply means to *'pause'*. It sounds quite easy doesn't it? Just **pause**…think amber traffic lights. It also acts as a prelude to stop - like at a red light. The trouble with **pausing** is that it can be deceptively difficult. We all know that once you get started it can be really hard to stop.

Remember Newton's law of motion (really Krishna's law!);

> *Every object in a state of uniform motion tends to remain in that state of motion unless an external force is applied to it.*

This definition reminds me of something my 'good old' Australian mum used to say. *"Just, don't get me started…"* We five kids knew what that meant. It was a warning. If you make Mum mad…you could be 'in for it' which translates as you'd better stop it or you'll get what we used to call an 'ear bashing.' 'Ear bashing' as interpreted by Cambridge Dictionary online, is slang for *angry words spoken to someone who has done something wrong'*.

So Back to Pause

"He who is slow to anger is better than the mighty; and he who rules his spirit, better than he who captures a city."

– PROVERBS 16:32

In the context of resolving relationship conflicts, to pause is certainly golden. Have you ever found yourself just about to slide down the precarious slopes of a conflict thinking… "Danger! Danger! I've been here before. I know if I say what I really want to say, we'll end up going down that same old road together. It won't be pretty, but I **need** to be heard. Oh who cares anyway?" You throw caution to the wind and dive head-long into an ever-escalating conflict that you just can't put the brakes on.

First Become Conscious

In the five drop remedy process, **pause** emerges first, and for good reason. Once you understand the fundamental value of this drop you will become motivated to use it. Simply put, it means understanding that when you 'lose it'…you really do *'lose it!'* You lose your temper, your dignity and your self-respect. Lastly, and not insignificantly, you really **do** lose the argument. As Dale Carnegie so aptly noted in his book 'How to Win Friends and Influence People; *'A man convinced against his will is of the same opinion still.'*

Srila Prabhupada often reminded us that we first need to become conscious before we can become *Krishna conscious*. Awareness is the first step. Once you are conscious or aware, you are more likely to choose the right action.

We have all heard a million times that the mode of passion ends in distress. We have not only heard it but we have also experienced it…probably more often than we would like to admit. Anger is a symptom of the mode of passion and ignorance. It is born from false ego and is dangerous on the path of Bhakti. Often described in a variety of heat-related terms like 'blazing', 'explosive' or 'burning' anger has the innate power to destroy.

Srila Prabhupada describes anger's effects perfectly in his Bhagavad-Gita As It Is purport…

"Akrodha means to check anger. Even if there is provocation one should be tolerant, for once one becomes angry his whole body becomes polluted. Anger is a product of the mode of passion and lust, so one who is transcendentally situated should check himself from anger."

– BHAGAVAD-GITA 16-1-3 PURPORT

Of course, we know there exists another type of anger, termed *'transcendental anger'*. This is the anger Hanuman displayed when he set fire to Ravana's city, Lanka. But let's not kid ourselves. Our anger is usually far from the transcendental kind. It is right up there along with lust and greed as one of the foremost enemies on the spiritual path. Aristotle puts it nicely;

"Anyone can become angry - that is easy, but to be angry with the right person at the right time, and for the right purpose and in the right way - that is not within everyone's power and that is not easy."

– ARISTOTLE - ANCIENT GREEK PHILOSOPHER

Triggers and Patterns

The beginning of any conflict is a critical point. We can either diffuse it or feed it; thus causing it to quickly dissolve or to escalate wildly.

This is the crucial moment when your buttons or triggers have been activated and you're ready to respond, all too often in a way that doesn't serve you or anyone else very well.

We all have triggers that 'set us off'. What my husband and I have discovered in our relationship is that these triggers often indicate patterns that we have developed and cemented over time. Every relationship has patterns. Patterns are not intrinsically negative. In fact, lots of them are positive and nurturing. Some however, *are* undesirable and can be damaging. Sadly, we can plod along for years acting out these dysfunctional patterns while naively wondering why our life is so marred by conflict and strife.

Let me share a relevant example; our *'map problem'*. My husband and I played out this ridiculous pattern for over 15 years before we finally had the good sense to pause and examine what was really going on.

*Life was not always fun when we went somewhere new. There was this expectation that I should be the one to navigate while my husband did the driving. I was a lousy navigator and I knew it (albeit, somewhere deep down)...I'm one of those spatially challenged people who has to turn maps upside down to make sense of them. Our pattern was that we would start out hopeful.... maybe this time it will work! However, I soon became tense and my husband often exasperated when I couldn't get the directions right. This inevitably led us into an attack/defend mode. Then one day as we headed down that old familiar path of conflict, we had the good sense to **pause**. "Hey....this is not working...in fact it has never worked.... Why are we doing this to ourselves?"*

There are a myriad of issues that can trigger conflict patterns. Often they revolve around genuine but sensitive concerns in areas such as spiritual standards like... do we eat in restaurants? Or role-expectations like... who puts the kids to bed, etc. On their own, these issues may seem minor, even insignificant, and that is why we hesitate to even bother dealing with them. If left unresolved however, they pile up, surfacing time and time again, just begging to be addressed and 'laid to rest'.

Dealing with Patterns – What's Your Style?

Until we achieve transcendence, social conditioning from our past tends to dictate how we deal with our conflict patterns. How we react in these situations can often be traced back to what was modelled by our parents. Even though we swear through clenched teeth that we will never act like our father/mother, when we don't have alternative methods, we may unconsciously revert to past conditioning.

For example, in your home the following strategies for dealing with conflict could have been;

Avoidance/Suppression... just keep the peace at any cost... clam up, give the silent treatment or as a last resort, cry.

Avoidance and suppression were prevalent in my childhood home...we all learnt to keep the peace to pacify a very 'explosive' father. The clear, but unspoken mantra was... don't do anything to make dad mad!

Confrontation/Combat - Perhaps this was the trend in your childhood... maybe in your house it was normal to argue your point, fight it out, shout, rave on, scream, etc.

Can you see how we often unconsciously bring our baggage with us without considering if it really even serves us?

When we think about it, our responses to conflict are nearly always protective in nature. Regardless of our conflict style, we are either attacking or defending our position or point of view. The problem with this instinctive preservation strategy is that nobody wins. You accuse me, I defend. Then I accuse you and you defend, even more passionately. So it goes, round and round, on and on.

The Price of anger – Why we lose so much when we 'lose it'!

Yudhisthira explains to Queen Draupadi in the epic Mahabharata...

> *"Only fools praise anger, considering it equivalent to energy. The wise keep anger at a distance. The man consumed by anger does not easily acquire generosity, dignity, courage, skill or the other attributes possessed by men of character. The wise consider him a man of character who restrains his wrath."*

– MAHABHARATA 1.24 KRISHNA DHARMA DASA

Dysfunctional behaviours repeated over time, compound into habits. The habit of dancing with anger is both dangerous and insidious. It effectively breaks down trust and eventually bankrupts our relationships.

Calm Is Strength

A valuable mantra I learnt in a classroom management course, which immediately resonated with me and has also served me well in many other areas of life, is 'Calm is Strength'. Have you ever noticed that as soon as you get angry, the other person stops focusing on the issue or problem at hand and begins to *focus on, and react to, your anger?* By getting upset you lose your power, by remaining calm you keep your power, as well as the respect of others. By remaining calm you also keep the focus on the real issue. This is big... ***really big!*** Please don't underestimate this principle. Once you understand it fully, it acts as a prime motivator that propels you into *pause* and inspires you to 'keep your cool'.

I have memories of losing my power when dealing with my own kids. I would be angrily raving away about something trivial, sounding very much like my dear mother. Then I would notice my kids' faces. Expressions of awful fascination mixed with a little fear. Sometimes there was even a hint of a defiant smile. It was like they knew they had won the battle when mum went slightly ballistic. Yes, and I can see that it must have been weirdly amusing watching their usually serene mother acting like a two year old having a tantrum.

On my side of the fence, initially it felt great to release and 'let it all out'. But as soon as I regained some semblance of calm, I was flooded with a mixture of guilt, shame and remorse. I truly felt like the evil witch. This is definitely a typical indicator of the effects of the mode of passion… feels good in the beginning… ends in suffering!

My children *'reacted'* to my anger according to their individual natures. My son, quiet and stubborn, would storm out without a word. My daughter, expressive and emotional, would match my anger with hers. Later, I would apologise for my outburst. After all I *was* supposed to be the adult. I didn't want to set a bad example. Of course, this reflection was to my credit; but the issue itself, however important, was lost, at least for the moment. I had surrendered my power because I had lost my temper.

Don't Be a 'Source of Dread'

"I first learned the concepts of nonviolence in my marriage."

– MAHATMA GANDHI

In the fourth canto of Srimad-Bhagavatam, Svyambhuva Manu advises his grandson, Dhruva Maharaja, to give up his anger and stop killing the Yakshas who had killed his brother.

He told Dhruva;

> "A person who desires liberation from this material world should not fall under the control of anger because when bewildered by anger one becomes a source of dread for all others."
>
> – SRIMAD-BHAGAVATAM 4.11.32

Our angry patterns often transform us into *sources of dread* for others. This brings only guilt and shame. It powerfully illustrates the need to learn to pause, change our state and remain calm.

The 'Calm Is Strength' mantra in action!

Keeping calm even under provocation is a symptom of our ascending to the human platform.

Srila Prabhupada constantly reminds us to become *dhira*... sober and gentle.

> "So dhiranam vartma. Because people must be first of all gentle. Then talk of Krsna and God consciousness. If he is an animal, what he can understand? This is Vedic system. Dhiranam. Dhira means must be gentle, perfectly gentle."
>
> –SRIMAD-BHAGAVATAM LECTURE 1.3.13
> LOS ANGELES, SEPTEMBER 18, 1972

In our personal relationship dynamic, my husband is often the more emotionally expressive one. I am the quiet, stubborn type that always tries to avoid conflict and would much prefer to retreat into stony silence. While I had been working on how to express myself, my husband had also been working on practicing *'calm is strength'*.

Have you ever noticed that whenever you work on improving yourself, Krishna tends to test you... *enter conflict.* I cannot honestly remember what it was all about, which is a lesson in itself. However, I **do** remember that we were both upset and that I had defaulted to my habitual 'silent treatment' strategy.

At this point I was fully expecting my husband to get *'expressive'.* But to my surprise, instead of letting me know just how angry he was...he walked calmly out the door. If he had left in anger, I would have focused on his angry state and felt even more justified in my stance. His leaving in this calm, un-energised manner afforded me space to ponder my part in the disagreement. What had I done that had contributed to the conflict? After a while I even became a little anxious. Where had he gone...I hoped he wasn't too upset?

My husband was only gone for an hour, but by the time he returned, I had entered into a more reflective and rational place. I was ready to listen to him and even ready to apologise for my part in the misunderstanding.

In accordance with our 'golden rule', we still worked through the issue (whatever it was) to the end, but now without raised voices or anger. Afterwards, we discussed and confirmed the realisation that practising **'calm is strength'** was a huge piece in solving the conflict puzzle. I did not lose respect for my husband when he walked out of the argument to protect his composure. On the contrary, I admired and respected him for it.

When a Pause is Longer

It's important to understand that **'pause'** (even though it sounds kind of short) can be as long as it takes to effectively 'drop the flame'. Asking how long it takes to 'pause' is something like asking 'how long is a piece of string'? It depends. Sometimes it can be as brief as a few seconds. However there are times when we need longer to drop the heat.

It's important to realise that it will be difficult to get to the next 'drop' (Drop Two Reflection) until you are in a place of reason and calm. So, take as long as you need. Remember though, we are not talking about avoiding the issue, pretending everything is fine and brushing it over. That is not calm...that is repression... and you'll find out just how dangerous that is in chapter four.

I remember once being angry and theoretically knowing I needed to pause so that I could progress to reflection. Seething, I muttered to my husband between clenched teeth, "I've paused but I'm far too angry to even **want** to go to the next step! The last thing I want is to see how *'it is'* for you!" It was at this point I realised that all I really needed was more time out...more space to retreat and effectively 'drop the flame'. My husband agreed. I went for a long walk, managed to calm down and started to see things more clearly. A few hours later we were able to talk rationally and were both ready to move into reflection. One size does not fit all. Sometimes just a brief pause is all that is needed, but at other times your *'pause'* may need to be longer. Again, pause *does not* mean we suppress our feelings, sweep it all under the rug and pretend nothing happened!

Using this *'Calm is Strength'* technique to pause and keep calm, in even the most difficult circumstances, naturally grants the mind 'reprieve' from its state of upset and allows you to regain your focus.

Be in Your Heart not Your Head

"The easiest way to please Krishna…simply you require your heart."

–SRILA PRABHUPADA CLASS MAYAPUR 1977

In times of conflict our greatest challenge is to learn how to be in our hearts and not in our heads; or as we used to preach to each other back in the old days, *"Just get off the mental platform!"* Instead of heeding the ego-boosting ramblings of the mind, we will find peace and tranquility in the core of our hearts, where we hold our highest intentions, thoughts and aspirations.

To be able to quickly press our personal *'Pause button'* it's important to be able to first notice what's going on, first in our mind and body and then learn to access our heart. This is where the *atma* and *paramatma* both reside. Krishna as Supersoul **wants** to direct our intelligence. In Bhagavad-gita it is described that according to our desire, Krishna grants us knowledge, remembrance or forgetfulness. When we are in the modes of passion and ignorance we cannot access our higher self. When we learn to access the mode of goodness by learning to pause and listen, we will be able to hear and tune into our good intelligence and be empowered to make the best Krishna Conscious decisions.

Seven Ways to Drop The Flame

Now that you have understood the importance of this first step, the following strategies will aid you in this key principle of keeping your cool. We have given you a smorgasbord of strategies to choose from. Select the ones that resonate best with you and are most applicable to your circumstances.

Call Your Best Friend!

Once, Srila Prabhupada advised Hayagriva dasa to call out to Krishna when he was having trouble with Mr. Lust. So why shouldn't we call out to Krishna when we have trouble with Mr. Lust's close friend, Mr. Anger! Too often, we ignore our real best friend, Krishna. Changing our state or mode is all about taking shelter of Krishna. Although calling out to Krishna is sometimes the hardest thing to do, it is the ultimate state-changer.

At our own initiation ceremony in Melbourne, April 1976, Srila Prabhupada urged us to pray to Krishna whenever Maya tries to deviate us.

"So, when there is some endeavour by Maya, just pray to Krishna - Please save me. I am surrendered, fully surrendered. Kindly give me protection. And Krishna will give you protection."

Take a Deep Breath...

Slow and conscious deep breathing can also help you to change your state, especially in the heat of the moment. When we get angry our breath naturally shortens and becomes shallow and hard. Think of the anger of Dhruva Maharaja when he was insulted by his stepmother, Suruchi. Anger induces short, sharp breathing which tightens up the whole body. Deep breathing counteracts the fight or flight stress reaction that underlies anger. Deliberately taking slow, deep breaths not only brings a soothing sense of relaxation, but also helps us to bring our attention back to the present moment.

Get Healthy!

"He who is regulated in his habits of eating, sleeping, recreation and work can mitigate all material pains by practicing the yoga system."

– BHAGAVAD-GITA 6.17

It is also crucial that we nurture our material health as a powerful preventative measure. Self-care is both proactive and reactive in nature. It is something you need do in advance to prepare yourself, as well as something you need to practice 'in the moment' as part of this process.

Rohininandana dasa wrote an excellent article on the importance of keeping our health. The complete article can be found on the *www.krishna.com* website.

Prabhupada would always sign his letters, "I hope this meets you in good health." He was concerned that his disciples lead a healthy life, including cleanliness, exercise, and a proper diet. When an early disciple became ill, Prabhupada advised him, "Your first business is to look after your health, because if you don't feel well everything will be topsy-turvy." He would sometimes tell sick devotees to suspend work and take complete rest.

Having vibrant health can help us achieve more emotional and social stability. It is favourable for the execution of our devotional service and should never be neglected or seen as *'maya'*.

Anger can be a symptom of an overstressed system. One devotee related to us that whenever she tried to talk to her husband about important issues he would become irritable and tense. What we found when working through the problem together with the couple, was that the wife would always bring up these 'important issues' just before bedtime. After a long day of physical work her husband was totally exhausted and the last thing he wanted to hear was problems. As soon as they recognised this unhealthy pattern, the couple were able to proactively avoid conflict by making a better time to discuss their problems.

Become Regulated!

We cannot expect to be in a calm and peaceful state without the strength that steady, daily sadhana gives us.

If we are regulated and have strong sadhana, we will be predominantly influenced by Sattva guna. When things aren't going our way and anger attempts to rear its ugly head, our material frustrations and hankerings will not have the power to bother us as much.

One essential key to keeping regulated is to make sure you get to bed early. If you don't get to bed early there is little chance of waking up early (no rocket science there!) When we get that early start, worshipping and chanting in the Brahma-Muhurta hour, our whole day becomes auspicious.

> "In the early morning hours (known as brahma-muhurta) one should get up and immediately chant the Hare Krsna mantra, or, at least, "Krsna, Krsna, Krsna." In this way one immediately becomes auspicious and transcendental to the infection of material qualities."
>
> **– CAITANYA-CARITAMRTA, MADHYAM LILA 24:331**

One way to get up early, is to trick the mind and tell yourself that you can have a power nap later in the day. Whether you get to the nap or not, you have defeated your mind and got yourself moving. Power naps of around 20-30 minutes can be energy building when needed. Be careful of long naps. It's all about those *'modes of nature'* again. When we sleep too much during the day we will be more susceptible to the mode of ignorance. We also interrupt our natural body clock and end up staying up too late which leads to …you guessed it…sleeping in the next morning. This late to bed, late to rise cycle is one that often delivers a death knell to good sadhana.

Head for the hills

While sorting out issues and being able to express how we feel is important, it is often counterproductive and downright dangerous when you are angry. Sometimes, what we need is time-out and a little breathing space in a more soothing environment.

Changing our environment is a powerful aid to changing our state. If a brief respite is all you need to cool down, just go into the next room. When I was a child and my little sister would annoy me, I would find sanctuary hiding in a little used closet. It was my own private refuge and I even had a torch hanging from a rope so that I could read my books there in peace.

So, for me, when the temperature gets too hot and I need a solid pause, I usually head out the door. Ayurveda teaches that anywhere with water, like streams, rivers or beaches will help calm and soothe an agitated mind. Sometimes it's wise to proactively locate a few calm-inducing retreats near where you live.

The most important point to remember when using a change of environment as a 'pause' strategy, is to *never, never,* and did I say *'never'*, leave with a parting flourish of anger. You will have to control yourself here and may need to *'white knuckle'* it. No door slamming or explosive, retreating remarks or gestures, because when you exit in a temper tantrum you will have automatically surrendered your power. The last impression your husband/wife will have to focus on is the angry state in which you left the house.

Get Out the Broomstick and Shoes!

There is sound reason to heed Srila Bhaktisiddhanta Sarasvati Thakura's allegorical advice, that in the morning our first business is to beat the mind with shoes one hundred times, and before retiring, a hundred times with a broomstick. This does not mean, however, that we ruthlessly beat our minds up with a barrage of negative self-talk.

The contemporary and popular term, *'self-talk'* may sound a bit 'new agey', but have you, like me, ever noticed that there is always some kind of chatter going on in your mind? We do indeed 'self-talk'. The elderly Gujarati Mahavishnu Maharaja often joked that our mind is like a zoo. Once we recognise that we are constantly talking to ourselves, mostly in a negative way, we can consciously choose a more positive and empowering dialogue.

Bhakti Tirtha Swami illustrates the destructive nature of the mind's negative self-talk in his book Spiritual Warrior.

People who always position themselves as the victim will never grow. They always think that other people are hurting them in some way. Although it could be a reality, if they anticipate and look for it, they will just create that around them to an even greater extent. They will begin to chant the same mantra in their minds, "Somebody didn't treat me right, someone didn't look at me right, someone didn't address me right, someone didn't take care of me properly, someone used me improperly..." Consequently, a person who always sees him or herself as the victim becomes the perpetual victim because violence brings more violence.

When you realise the huge impact your self-talk can make, resolve to use it as a more positive and encouraging force.

Visualize your way to Success

Sitting on a park bench in New York City, Srila Prabhupada, in conversation with an acquaintance stated, *"We have so many temples, so many devotees, so many books.....there is just some time separating us."*

Visualizations are similar to, and often build upon, self-talk. It's actually the art of transposing our positive self-talk into a vision. Like Srila Prabhupada on that park bench, we can use our minds to generate what we want, and to actually visualise or see it happening. It is often quoted that the mind can be a friend or a powerful enemy of the conditioned soul. *Intentional* and positive visualisations can purposefully direct our mind and help us achieve our goals.

Self talk and Visualization in Action

I use both positive self-talk and visualisation in my teaching practice. I visualise all the activities I have prepared for the children going exactly according to plan. When I find myself stressing I check in with w*hat my mind* is saying. If it's not positive I catch myself and change it.

One day I casually mentioned to a close friend how I was totally exhausted because some children in my class were 'draining' me. "Can you hear yourself?", he said. It took me a few seconds to tune into what he was saying. Then I got it. It became clear that I was letting this negative self-talk dictate my mood. I was accepting and preparing myself for a day of 'draining' children. I even saw 'draining children' in my head. Immediately I changed my mind-set and dropped the 'draining' word from my vocabulary. Instead I chose to see those previously 'draining' kids as 'lively and intelligent'. I now visualized having fun with a group of lively, intelligent children. It made the world of difference to my mood and my day.

OK...Now I've calmed down... what next?

Drop One 'Drop the Flame' works brilliantly to take the heat out of any upset. However practicing how to 'pause' is only the first of a five drop process; it isn't meant to stand alone like some kind of 'miracle cure'. Rather, it provides us with an effective 'entry point' to the next step, Drop the Vain. This is where we begin to consider the other person and how they are being impacted by what's happening.

Key Points from Chapter One - Drop the Flame (Pause)

- Understand the importance of 'pause' and you will be motivated to use it. The main point to remember here is that it is impossible to work through conflict when you are under the grip of anger.

- **Recognise your specific triggers and patterns.** Once you do, you will be able to put the brakes on and prevent yourself from going down that well-trodden path of conflict. Just as in our 'map problem' example, you may realise that this is a negative pattern that you keep playing out.

The difference is that with these new tools you can finally do something about it!

- **Know the real price of anger** and why you really do 'lose it' when you lose it. This is pivotal. Remember what you lose when you dance with anger. You lose your respect, your reasoning and instead of focusing on the issue or problem at hand, your spouse will focus on and react to your anger. It is totally lose/lose.

- **Understand and be motivated to practise 'Calm is Strength'.** You keep your power when you keep calm, even in the face of conflict. Once you fully realise this you will be motivated to do whatever it takes to keep your cool.

- **Pick and choose seven ways to 'drop the flame'.** Try the ones that resonate with you first, then gradually experiment with them all.

CHAPTER 2

Drop the Vain (Reflection)

It's Not Just About You!

When faults in others misguide and delude you- Have patience, introspect, find faults in yourself. Know that others cannot harm you unless you harm yourself.

– QUOTE BY BHAKTISIDDHANTA SARASVATI THAKURA

We have a mirror image inserted in the graphic symbol for Drop Two, entitled, 'Drop the Vain'. There are two messages implied in this symbol. A vain person is someone who always thinks of himself; thus the mirror imprint on the symbol. In contrast, the mirror image demonstrates a positive symbol of reflection, which essentially means the ability to empathise and reflect back what others are thinking and feeling.

If we want nourishing and reciprocal relationships we need to practice reflection. Instead of being fixated solely on ourselves we need to become more like a mirror by trying to understand and accurately reflect the other person's point of view back to them.

Go Deeper!

Reflecting is favourable to spiritual consciousness and acts as an invitation to function at a higher level. It urges us to go deeper. From my observations, some people seem naturally blessed with this skill. Others, like me, whose default setting is firmly wedged in ego, need to consciously develop it through steady practice. Either way, once we grasp its importance we will appreciate that being able to empathise and reflect, really is a magic key, one that opens the door to dissolving conflicts quickly and painlessly.

What About Me?

When we fail to reflect and get stuck in the 'me' syndrome we create and perpetuate unhealthy communication patterns.

These behaviour patterns that predict divorce have been well researched and studied. One famous study is by Dr. Gottman, who painstakingly identified the most corrosive communication and behaviour patterns; naming them the gloomy, *"Four Horsemen of the Apocalypse."*

These deadly communication patterns are worth being aware of. They typically indicate a lack of reflection, which ultimately springs from this 'all about me' mentality.

- **Criticism:** stating one's complaints as a defect in one's partner's personality, i.e., giving the partner negative trait attributions. Example: "You always talk about yourself. You are so selfish." This is a very negative and destructive behaviour pattern, but unfortunately it is very common and slowly but surely kills the relationship.

- **Contempt:** statements that come from a relative position of superiority. Contempt is the greatest predictor of divorce and must be eliminated. Example: "You're an idiot." Contempt is a mood and is essentially the culmination of all criticism.

- **Defensiveness:** self-protection in the form of righteous indignation or innocent victim-hood. Defensiveness wards off a perceived attack. Example: "It's not my fault that we're always late; it's your fault." This one is caused by a lack of reflection and leads to the victim mentality. It leaves us trapped in the viscous cycle of 'attack and defend'.

- **Stonewalling:** emotional withdrawal from interaction. Example: The listener does not give the speaker the usual nonverbal signals that the listener is "tracking" the speaker. Stonewalling shows hopelessness in the relationship. There is no connection and therefore no interest in communicating.

Can you see yourself in any of the above? If you have identified any of these as patterns, you do need to be concerned about the health of your relationship.

The Price of Being Right

We all have a thirst for knowledge. Our original, spiritual nature is described as *sat, cit, ananda,* full of eternity knowledge and bliss. Unfortunately, influenced by the modes of material nature and contaminated by our false ego, we become desperate to dominate, to prove that we are always right. We thus strive to control...something, anything. This often shows up in our relationships.

We all hold different opinions and perspectives because we are all individuals. Some of us are definitely more opinionated than others. This can be a powerful quality when used correctly, but sometimes it can pose a dangerous threat to the harmony of our relationships.

Srila Prabhupada would laugh heartily when telling the story of the scissors and the knife. This story illustrates the futility of using force when trying to get your point across. Suhotra Swami retells it here:

This is a story often told by Srila Prabhupada called "Scissors philosophy". This story illustrates stubbornness ...when someone only sees his own point of view. So two men were having an argument, they wanted to cut something and they argued about which is the best tool to use to cut with. One was saying: "Knife, for this thing a knife is better." And the other was saying: "No, scissors." So back and forth, one says: "Knife!" the other says "Scissors." It became a very heated argument. Then finally the one who was advocating the knife, he said: "If you don't agree with me, I'll throw you in the river". And the other one said: "I'll never change my mind". So then the knife man, he picked up the scissors man and threw him in the river. And the scissors man, he couldn't swim so he was starting to drown and the knife man said: "Look, if you agree with me, then I will come and save you." So as the scissors man was going down for the third time he put his hand out of the water and went like this (showing scissors with his fingers).

So next time you find yourself stuck in this stubborn, need to be right attack/defend cycle, remember the fate of the scissors man!

Change Your Mood...

The simple truth is that we hold people in relationship with the idea of experiencing love. Relationships with devotees, whether husband, wife, friend, parent or child are all meant to be based on loving service and reciprocation. Srila Prabhupada termed this, the 'mood of cooperation'. He practically begged us, time and time again to imbibe this Vaisnava mood, so that our whole movement would continue to thrive and flourish.

It is no secret that even on a material level, to nourish and maintain successful relationships you need to develop a loving mood of giving.

Indradumnya Swami relates an experience about how he was once on a flight and encountered a couple in their 90s. They were heading out to celebrate their 75th wedding anniversary. Maharaja took the opportunity to ask them how they had maintained such a long-lasting relationship.

"I am often the priest for many weddings, and I also give many wedding speeches. So could you please tell me, what are some words of advice that I can give to newlyweds? What has held you both together for so long, and so happily?"

Spontaneously they replied in unison:

"Just give more than you take."

Our Deep Yearning...

We all have a deep yearning to be understood. That is why we feel justified to act in certain ways and why it troubles us deeply when our intentions are questioned. "If only this person would tune into me and ***really*** try and understand me," we anguish mentally.

We even use the term *'mis-understanding'* to describe a conflict. And most of the time that's exactly what it is - a *mis*-understanding! Our biggest problem is that we find it difficult to get 'out of our own heads' to gain a more authentic perspective. All too often, we rush ahead and invent a story in our minds about what we ***think*** our husband/wife or friend meant, and we consequently react to that fabricated story... any wonder we experience conflict?

What do you mean... who left the lid loose!

Our fabricated mental stories tend to congregate mostly around issues or circumstances that we are oversensitive about. I will give you a very minor example that illustrates this. By the way, it is often these seemingly trivial incidents that compound into these negative patterns that we keep talking about. One close devotee friend who has been practising the 5 drop formula for some time, described the huge meaning she inserted into her husband's passing comment.

"I am often in a rush (influenced by the mode of passion) and tend to be a little careless about things. Because I was labelled 'a dreamer' and 'lazy' as a child, I am also highly sensitive about anything that insinuates this. Once my husband was joking about who could possibly have left the top loose on a jar of peanut butter. I took his casual remark personally – it struck a chord somewhere deep down; here it was all over again. I was a dreamer and a lazy one at that. I gave him my best (or worst) withering look and retaliated sharply.

My husband was bewildered that his comment had triggered such a disproportionate reaction in me. Once we worked through the problem and he finally understood where I was coming from, he could then empathise with me and understand my reaction. From my side once I felt understood, I could then appreciate that my husband's comment was not coming from a 'bad' place and could finally put it into perspective. I know that leaving lids loose on peanut butter jars is not a 'hanging offence' although maybe it was something I needed to address. However it was actually me who made the big deal out of the whole thing! After all it was just a loose lid on a peanut butter jar, for goodness sake, not a major crime, but I had given it so much meaning. In other words it was I who had caused my own suffering!"

So whenever you find yourself overreacting to someone's casual comments, go deeper; look inside and see what meaning you might be adding to the event.

Reflect... or Stay Stuck

We have met the enemy and he is us.

– WALT KELLY - POGO

When we get fixated in our version of events or how it is for us, we become stuck – unable to progress towards any kind of resolution. Resolutions never happen unless there is a shift. This next statement is absolutely true, so take note!

Every time we have successfully resolved a misunderstanding someone has made this shift (consciously or unconsciously) into reflection. It really is that 'black and white' – no shift equals no resolution.

So as Srila Prabhupada used to quip… 'What is the difficulty?'

Well, just because it's *simple,* doesn't mean it's easy. Then again… getting into reflection **would** be easy if we could only get our self-ego out of the way! This is when I realise that we are tragically our own *'worst enemy'.*

Our refusal to reflect and empathise comes at a heavy cost. It causes us to either suppress our feelings or to perpetuate the vicious cycle of attack/defend. This wears everyone down and worst of all it often gets ugly. We say things we don't really mean. We want to hurt because we are hurt. There is no benefit in this lose/lose scenario. The tricky part is that once we board this emotional roller-coaster (Newton's Law of Motion again), it takes on a life of its own and is very hard to stop.

Love ...not Force

There is a world of difference between guiding with love and controlling with force. The recipient can certainly feel the difference. A husband is expected to offer spiritual guidance to his wife. Parents need to guide their children. As a teacher I also have the responsibility of guiding my students. The problem occurs when we insist and rely on force and control.

In an early morning walk conversation in Hawaii of 1974, Srila Prabhupada offers the secret ingredient to any relationship...love.

Devotee: *We have the choice of being controlled either by love or by force.*

Srila Prabhupada: *Yes. When we decide to be controlled by Krishna, it is out of love for Him. Similarly, you are being controlled by me, but there is no force. You serve me voluntarily, out of love. I am not paying you; still, when I ask you to do something you immediately do it. Why? There is love between us.*

Don't settle for less!

The *love not force,* principle is the foundation for all successful relationships. Yes, we can serve our husband/wife out of a sense of duty without love, but we need not settle for this. It is vital to act in such a way as to always keep the love and affection in your relationship healthy and alive! You are already heavily invested in your relationship, but force will only maim and ultimately kill it.

Srila Prabhupada also advised our Gurukula teachers to use love instead of force, indicating that force is impersonal.

"It is not something mechanical process, if we force in such a way they will come out like this, no. We are persons, and Krishna is a Person, and our relationship with Krishna, He leaves open as a voluntary agreement always, and that voluntary attitude--Yes, Krishna, I shall gladly co-operate whatever you say--that ready willingness to obey is only possible if there is love. Forcing will not make me agree. But if there is love, oh, I shall gladly do it. That is bhakti, that is Krishna Consciousness."

– LETTER TO: RUPA VILASA HYDERABAD 18 NOVEMBER, 1972

Opening the Door to Authentic Communication

"Our Society is like one big family and our relationships should be based on love and trust. We must give up the fighting spirit and use our intelligence to push ahead. You should accept help from your Godbrothers."

– SP LETTER TO UPENDRA 8/6/70

Healthy communication is fundamental to maintaining harmonious relationships and is crucial to our progress in spiritual life.

Over the years we have seen many devotees leave the association of devotees as a result of conflict and miscommunication. Yes, we **do** need to find another way, but new alternatives can only be generated when we learn how to listen, to seek to understand the other person's point of view and to empathise with them.

It is said that God granted us two ears but only one mouth for an obvious reason. Our experience confirms that we do much better in relationships and life in general, when we listen twice as much as we speak.

One of Stephen Covey's 7 *Habits of Highly Effective People is First Seek to Understand, Then to Be Understood.*

RELATIONSHIP RESCUE REMEDY

The sequence in the above aphorism is also important. Once we feel understood then we become open and ready to listen.

As Covey puts it, *"Just as a person who is drowning can only think of getting air and nothing else, in the same way until a person feels understood it is very hard for them to listen. Being understood is like accessing 'psychological air'."*

Be First into Reflection

A crucial point to understand when resolving our day to day conflicts, is that it doesn't matter who makes the decision to shift into reflection mode first. Sometimes we feel reluctant to be the first one to reflect. Our thoughts may go something like this.

"Well, it's actually more her/his fault than mine, so it's only fair that they should reflect first." We somehow feel that by leaping into reflection first, we are accepting more of the blame. **This mentality is the illusion that keeps us stuck.** It may seem counter-intuitive but it just doesn't work like this. Resolving conflict starts by moving beyond the blame and shame cycle and trying to understand each other. Reflection is totally win/win. When I become reflective it opens the door for the other person to do the same. Then we both get what we want, which is fundamentally to be heard and understood.

Once the first person has been heard and understood, they feel free to let their guard down. The cycle of attack/defend has been shattered by the force of empathic listening. When this dynamic is firmly established, you will be in the race to see who can shift into reflection first!

Learn How to Listen

A wise old owl sat in an oak.
The longer he sat, the less he spoke.
The less he spoke, the more he heard.
Why can't we be like that wise old bird?

– NURSERY RHYME - AUTHOR UNKNOWN

It's hard to listen for most people. We want to talk. We want to tell people what to do, what not to do and what we think. In other words it's all about guess who? **Me!** This mentality reminds me of when I was a teenager and I would ask my friend how her weekend was. It was incredibly important as a teenager to have what we termed as a *'good'* weekend. However, even as my friend was enthusiastically recounting all the exciting things she had done, I would be frantically formulating and adjusting my response. In reality, I was waiting for her to finish so I could give my drastically enhanced version of what was really important in life … *my* weekend. Looking back I am amazed at how shallow and self-centred such listening was, but hey that's often where you are at when you are 15!

Now that most of us are somewhat older, and have gained adequate first-hand experience of the pains of misunderstanding and conflict, we may be ready to develop and enhance our existing listening skills.

How Empathic Listening Works

Empathic listening, often called active or reflective listening, creates a culture of trust and a climate for healthy resolution. It helps us to build strong relationships based upon mutual respect, appreciation and trust.

There are many excellent books that outline the steps of effective listening. They are worth reading.

Here is a nutshell summary gleaned from one such book: *Listening, The Forgotten Skill* by Madelyn Burley-Allen that will help you get started -

1. **Be attentive.** Be interested and alert. Show your attentiveness through nonverbal (body language) behaviour such as facial expressions and hand gestures.

2. **Indicate you are listening by providing brief,** noncommittal acknowledging responses, e.g., "Yes", "Uh-huh," "I see." Give non- verbal acknowledgements such as head nodding, facial expressions that match the speaker. Use an open and relaxed body position and maintain eye contact.

3. **Be a sounding board.** Allow the speaker to bounce ideas and feelings off you, all the while assuming a non-judgmental, non-critical manner.

4. **Avoid asking lots of questions.** This sends the message of cross-examining the speaker. Be like a mirror - simply reflect back what you think the speaker is *saying and feeling* for clarification purposes.

5. **Don't discount the speaker's feelings** by using typical and condescending phrases like "It's not so bad," or "You'll get over it."

6. **Never allow the speaker to trigger you.** This happens when you allow yourself to get involved in an argument, or you accuse or pass judgment on the other person. You invariably end up in an attack and defend mode.

7. **Offer invitations to say more,** e.g., "Tell me about it," or "I'd like to hear more about that."

8. **Adhere to good listening 'ground rules'.** Don't interrupt, change the subject, rehearse answers in your own head, give advice, teach/preach or move in a new direction.

9. ***Always* reflect back** to the speaker what you understand and how you think the speaker feels. Ask them to confirm your reflection. "So what you mean/how you felt is … ?"

Be a Mirror

Reflective listening is mindful and potent. It shows the other person that you understand and appreciate what is occurring for them. Just like the mirror illustrated in the graphic for this drop, we want to reflect back as accurately as we can without twisting the meaning.

When reflecting back we also have to be careful to avoid using autobiographical responses such as, *"I experienced the exact same thing… I know exactly how you feel."* Chances are things are not exactly the same as your situation and even if they are, everyone is likely to experience it differently on an emotional level.

If you think you had a similar experience you could ask *"Is it something like this?"* but more important is to tune into how they are feeling and experiencing the situation in this moment. When you get into 'empathy' with the other person, you will know it. They will express it both in words and body language.

The secret is to remain open and humble. *"I think I hear what you are saying… please correct me if I'm wrong."* Then attempt to repeat as close to verbatim as you can, what the other person just said about how they experienced whatever happened, and how it made them feel. If what you verbalise 'hits the spot' they will let you know. If not, they will also let you know. Your job is to keep adjusting your understanding until you get it right.

When We Stop Listening...

I was recently with a close friend who was relating a problem to me. I immediately slid into *'advice mode'*. I gave the best and most practical advice under the sun and I was truly impressed with myself. It was sensible...it was Krishna Conscious and it was valuable. But then I paused and glanced at my friend's face. My friend possesses a very expressive face and I knew instantly that I had lost her. I had shut her down with my well-meant guidance. It had literally gone over like the proverbial 'lead balloon'. I stopped and checked myself and was able to express this realisation to her. My friend is actually the best reflective listener I know, so she laughed and confirmed my suspicion.

A Time to Talk

At this point you might be thinking as I once thought. *"Well, hold on a minute here...what is the use of this! People need advice. We are preachers and we should give each other Krishna Conscious instruction. I mean that's what we're all about isn't it."* And you would be right...in a way.

There is a place for giving advice and counsel, but the rule is simple. Give your advice when someone asks you for it. If my friend had asked me for advice, my pearls of wisdom would have been much appreciated - but she wasn't **asking** for advice. She was simply sharing her thoughts and probably knew what to do herself. In this instance she didn't need or want my advice, she just wanted me to listen, to empathise and to be *'there'* for her.

Reflection.. The Essence

All the drops in the 5 Drop Rescue Remedy are important, but Drop the Vain (Drop 2) is especially pivotal. The first drop, *Drop the Flame*, leads into it and the next three drops flow on from it.

Our next drop (**Drop the Blame**) flows through every area of our lives. It's like the glue that binds all the drops together.

Key Points from Chapter Two - Drop the Vain (Reflect)

- **Realise it's not all about you!** There are two in a marital relationship. Our ego keeps us entrenched in our own heads and this shows up in our 'deadly' communication patterns. We need to consider others if our relationships are going to work, and learning to reflect is a key principle.

- **Understand the price of being right.** When we get stuck in the *'me'* syndrome we can argue about anything. Our arguments are often so futile and petty that we can sometimes recall the drama we created even years later, rather than what the conflict was about! Respecting other's opinions and viewpoints doesn't mean we have to give up our own, but when you are tempted to force your ideas or opinions upon others, just remember the fate of the scissors man!

- **When you fail reflect you remain stuck- so race to reflection!** No-one has ever resolved a conflict without reflecting how *'it is'* for the other person. You will never *lose* when you dive in and reflect first. When you understand that reflecting opens the door for your spouse to do the same, you will want to race to reflection.

- **Practice your empathic listening skills.** There are many good books on effective listening skills. Follow and practise the simple formula that we have outlined and you can't go wrong. The key word here is **practise!**

CHAPTER 3

Drop the Blame (Accept Responsibility)

"The chains that keep you bound to the past are not the actions of another person. They are your own anger, stubbornness, lack of compassion, jealousy and blaming others for your choices. It is not other people that keep you trapped; it is the entitled role of victim that you enjoy wearing. There is a familiarity to pain that you enjoy because you get a payoff from it. When you figure out what that payoff is then you will finally be on the road to freedom."

– SHANNON L. ALDER - CHRISTIAN RELATIONSHIP WRITER

Drop three of the 5 Drop Relationship Rescue Remedy teaches us how to accept total responsibility and thus end the tiresome *'blame game'* forever.

Who is responsible to make a relationship work?

In our 'Success In The Grihastha Ashram' workshops we always ask …

'So, whose responsibility is it to make a relationship work?'

"Is it the man? After all he is supposed to be the guide or leader. Or perhaps it's the woman? Surely, she should be the 'submissive' one... and after all isn't she supposed to be good at all this communication stuff?"

"Or could it be 50/50?" This option sounds by far the most fair and rational and it usually wins the largest vote.

We then suggest that **the best relationships thrive when both the man and the woman take 100% responsibility to do whatever it takes to make it work.** Now (like many of our participants) you might say that this sounds the same as 50/50... but it's not. There is no back door escape with this one. You can't say 'I've done my 50%... now it's your fault... if there's still a problem, you must be to blame. No, accepting 100% responsibility means full commitment from both sides.

Dropping the blame, involves being willing to accept personal responsibility to do whatever it takes to get through to the other side of any conflict. It's easy and convenient just to point the finger and blame others; but it's not so easy to accept responsibility.

We deeply fear that by accepting responsibility we might lose out and end up as the 'scapegoat'. We fear that accepting responsibility might be construed as an admission of our guilt, and that by accepting our part in the blame equation automatically minimises our spouse's contribution. Thankfully, it just doesn't work like this.

You are Responsible

The following is an anonymous letter about the power of accepting responsibility. It says it so well that we have laminated it and displayed it prominently in our house as a potent reminder.

Perhaps the most important personal choice you can make is to accept complete responsibility for everything you are and everything you will ever be. This is the great turning point in life.

The acceptance of personal responsibility is what separates the superior person from the average person. Personal responsibility is the pre-eminent trait of leadership and the wellspring of high performance in every person, in every situation.

The acceptance of complete responsibility for your life means that you refuse to make excuses or to blame others for anything in your life that you're not happy about. You refuse; from this moment forward, to criticize others for any reason. You refuse to complain about your situation, or about what has happened in the past. You eliminate all your "if only"s and "what if"s and focus instead on what you really want and where you are going.

From now on, no matter what happens, say to yourself, "I am responsible". If you are not happy with any part of your life, say, "I am responsible' and get busy changing it. If something goes wrong, accept responsibility and begin looking for a solution. If you are not happy with your current income, accept responsibility and begin doing those things that are necessary for you to increase it. If you are not happy with the amount of time you are spending [on your spiritual practices] and with your family, accept responsibility for that as well and begin doing something about it.

When you accept responsibility, you feel personally powerful. The acceptance of responsibility gives you a tremendous sense of control over yourself and your life. The more responsibility you accept, the more confidence and energy you have. The more responsibility you accept, the more capable and competent you feel.

The acceptance of responsibility is the foundation of high self-esteem, self-respect and personal pride [not false pride]. The acceptance of personal responsibility lies at the core of the personality of every outstanding man or woman.

On the other hand, when you make excuses, blame other people, complain or criticize, you give your power away. You weaken yourself and your resolve. You turn over control of your emotions to the people and situations you are blaming or complaining about.

You do not escape responsibility by attempting to pass it off onto other people. You are still responsible. But you give up a sense of control over your life. You begin to feel like a victim and see yourself as a victim. You become passive and resigned rather than powerful and proactive. Instead of feeling on top of your world, you feel as if your world was on top of you.

This way of thinking leads you up a blind alley, from which there is no escape. It is a dead end road on which you should refuse to travel.

Don't Be a Victim

"Victimhood is often the last stage before outright aggression."

– ANONYMOUS

The most destructive consequence from blaming is that it leaves you thinking, feeling, and acting like a victim. By blaming others, you give up your power. You then have no alternative than to assume and act like a victim.

I was once attempting to counsel a devotee who was having lots of conflict in her marriage. She was unable to shift her focus even a fraction from blaming her husband for everything that was going wrong in their relationship. I tried hard to get her to consider that she could possibly own a part in the equation, but she was so solidly entrenched in 'the blame game' that she couldn't, or wouldn't budge. Even if her husband was **more** at fault, her 'victim energy' was totally draining for both of us! I sadly concluded that no amount of counselling would benefit her. We can use simple logic to look at it like this- if it's *all* the other person's fault there is no chance of resolution. End of story. This is totally lose/lose.

Unfortunately my friend's stance didn't change and her relationship predictably crumbled. She remains consumed with bitterness to this day. My realisation; it's easy to blame others...but harder, much harder, to look at ourselves.

From Victim to Victory

Years ago another close friend of mine lost her husband...he left her and went off with her 'best friend'. My friend was devastated, but she ultimately took shelter of Krishna. When I think back, there were so many she could have blamed...her husband as first choice...the other woman...even ISKCON or Krishna for 'doing' this to her. I saw her go through the different stages of grief and anger. I noticed how attentive her chanting became - in fact she became 'renowned' in our temple for her deep and meditative japa. I was particularly awed when she was able to forgive both her husband and her best friend. I asked her once how she could do this. She laughed and related that at some point in the grief process she realised that blaming others simply increased her own suffering. She had tried it and had the good sense to understand that it was all-consuming and would eventually destroy her. She refused to be a victim and decided instead to take responsibility for her suffering and forgive everyone in the equation, including herself. My friend died just a few years later in a car accident. She blamed no one for anything and her death was glorious, with hand in bead bag and a heart free of malice or blame.

Moving Beyond Blame

Don't get drawn into the blame game; a game that no one can ever win. No-one benefits when we dwell on and painfully dissect who is at fault, or even who is *more* at fault. Accepting our part in the blame equation is a vital and essential step forward. It gets us back on track and has a major role in repairing and rebuilding relationships. When you take the courageous step of recognizing and owning the part *you* play, you can then access the power to change the situation, resolve the issue and move forward.

Discover Your Own Contribution

To avoid becoming a slave to the victim mentality, practice the following three important principles.

1: Realize that the only person you can change is yourself.

We would dearly love to have a magic wand that 'fixed' everyone. Unfortunately it doesn't work like this. Usually we drive ourselves and everyone else crazy trying to achieve this impossible task. One devotee related that when she finally gave up trying to 'fix' everyone in her life and just tried to work on herself, (which she soon discovered was enough on its own!), amazing things happened. Think about it like this...while you are trying to fix and run everyone else's life, who's fixing and running yours?

2: Could it be Your Problem?

Any time someone is pointing a finger at you, ask yourself what kernel of the accusation could actually be true. Be brutally honest with yourself, because (Lord forbid!) there may be a tiny grain of truth in the claim. I know that's a hard pill to swallow, but it is liberating and empowering to own your own stuff!

Sometimes the faults or shortcomings we see in others are the very ones we should be working on ourselves. Again, there must be a law about this somewhere and if there isn't, there should be!

Srila Prabhupada never entertained our complaining tendency. When devotees would write to him complaining about their Godbrothers/Godsisters, more often than not Srila Prabhupada would throw the responsibility back onto the complainer!

"If there is some incident and I claim that no one is cooperating with me or no one will work with me, that is MY defect, NOT THEIRS. The Vaisnava devotee must think like this. We should not find fault with others and criticise and go away. That is not the Vaisnava way. Better we should always be willing to offer all respect to others and consider them as our superiors always."

– LETTER TO GAURASUNDARA - AUGUST 26, 1972

3: Ask and You Shall Receive…

This one is simple but profound. If you don't know what you're contributing, simply ask the other person what you are doing, saying, (or failing to do or say). Consider that it might even be the way you are doing or saying it that could be impacting the other person in a negative way. I suffered with a very explosive father in my childhood and subsequently hate and want to immediately escape from raised, angry voices. To me it means stress of the worst kind. When I communicated these feelings to my husband, he was able to understand my sensitivity and has always made an effort to keep his voice calm and his tone even and low.

A Word of Caution…

When you ask, be prepared and open to really *hear* without getting defensive. Ask in a genuine way that doesn't trigger a defensive reaction. Your mood will be very important here, as you will be communicating not only with words but through your energy, voice tone and body language. Once you realise your contribution, you can then reflect how this is affecting the other person and work through the rest of the drops to resolve your issue.

Recognise the Real Problem

"There cannot be love without trust and there cannot be trust unless we take the responsibility to act in a way that people can trust us."

– RADHANATH SWAMI

Once you accept full responsibility for the issue, you will experience a most defining moment. You will realise that you and your spouse are both on the same side! Bingo! You are then left with the *issue* as the real 'problem' and not each other. This is a great relief and a key juncture in conflict resolution. You are now willing and able to completely exit the insidious attack/defend cycle which has kept you stuck for so long. From this new vantage point, problems start to melt away and trust can be re-built.

Love and Trust

Relationships built on a strong foundation of trust can weather many a storm. Years of constant bickering can erode this trust, breeding doubt and suspicion. Sometimes we even imagine that our partner is 'out to get us'. When you think about the underlying mentality that evokes such a feeling, it reveals a very negative and critical tendency. *It shows that you are thinking the worst about the other person, as well as yourself.* Think about it like this; by doubting their good intentions, you are being doubly unkind; unkind to them as well as to yourself. Stay with me here! How *you* are thinking *they* are thinking says volumes about how you think of yourself. For example, if you imagine that your spouse thinks you are incapable in some area… then what you are unconsciously suggesting is that you actually see *yourself* in this way.

This is when we need to remind ourselves to be kind… both to ourselves and to others. And don't worry if your 'trust account' is low or even overdrawn, we will show you how to re-generate, protect and nourish that trust in Drop Five (Pouring on the Energy).

The Mind... Friend or Enemy?

"For him who has conquered the mind, the mind is the best of friends; but for one who has failed to do so, his mind will remain the greatest enemy."

– BHAGAVAD-GITA 6.6

Another important point to remember in avoiding the blame game is that we sometimes give meanings to events that are not always factual. I used to think the Bhagavad-gita verse 2:14 *'matra-sparsas'* was more about tolerating bad weather or more physical types of tribulations. I now realise that the part *'arising from sense perception'* can also refer to how the mind filters our experiences. This filtering process gives rise to our consequent feelings of happiness or distress. This is why a particular event that gives distress to one may not cause it to another. This perception can be experienced either on the physical or mental plane, but it's intrinsically the mind's perception that causes our pleasure and pain.

Mean Meaning Machines

Day to day communication can hold a myriad of different meanings for us. Our partner may say something offhand and we immediately attach huge meaning to it. We have all been in this place on one end of the communication spectrum or the other. You say something, hoping for some understanding, but the other person in your life just doesn't get it. In fact, not only do they not *'get it'*, but they misinterpret your words and intentions and instead react to how you have made them *feel*.

I remember reading a great example of this from the Christian based relationship book, *Fascinating Womanhood* by Helen Andelin. A husband was fishing for a little appreciation from his wife about his earning ability. He casually commented about how hard it was to provide adequately for a family in these trying times. The wife mistook her husband's purpose and thought he was indirectly criticising her spending habits. *"Well, I hardly spend anything... it's been years since I had a new* dress." You can imagine how this comment went over to our heroic husband who was already sensitive about his earning capability and was hoping for a little acknowledgement. Yes, *'lead balloon'* comes to mind. And so it went on; with each trying desperately to justify their position and feel validated and understood. The husband in this scenario felt diminished and defeated, while his wife felt criticised and humiliated; and all by the filter of their fallible perception.

The Power of Perception

"In the material world, conceptions of good and bad are all mental speculations. Therefore, saying, 'This is good, and this is bad', is all a mistake."

– SRI CAITANYA-CARITAMRTA ANTYA 4.176

Perception is a vital component in nurturing the strength and stability of our relationships. For example many couples discover after a year or two of marriage that they are radically 'different' from their spouses. However, we could **choose** to see these differences in qualities and nature as either 'conflicting' or 'complementary'. Complementary is a much healthier, kinder and a more empowering perception. It means that we are certainly different, but that we complement each other! Imagine if you were *too* similar in nature to your spouse. Hmmm … two types of *me* … two types of *him* … that could get intense.

Perception can help us to see beyond the duality of circumstances in our life. A favourite well-known Chinese fable that illustrates the fragility of perception is one I think of whenever things don't seem to be going the way I think they *'should'*.

Good Luck, Bad Luck!

There was an old farmer who had a beautiful horse. This horse was not only his family's pride and joy, but it was also a means of income for the family.

One day, the horse ran away. Fellow villagers visited the old man to give their condolences for such a stroke of bad luck, as the loss of his horse represented a staggering financial blow that would be hard to recover from.

"Good luck, bad luck: Who can tell?" replied the old man. "It is as it is. My horse is gone."

Perplexed at the man's nonchalance towards the apparent tragedy, the villagers went about their business.

A few days later, the horse returned with a pack of 12 wild horses in tow. Again the villagers gathered, this time to offer their congratulations at such a stroke of good luck. Now he had 12 more horses with which to make 12 times the income! *What a godsend,* they said.

"Good luck, bad luck: Who can tell?" replied the old man again. "All I see is that 12 more horses have appeared."

The next week, while breaking in one of the wild horses, the old man's son fell and both his legs were broken. *What bad luck!* The villagers exclaimed. *Your son has broken both of his legs. That's terrible. How will you get your work done? You are too old to do it yourself.*

"Good luck, bad luck: Who can tell?" was the now predictable answer of the old man. "My son has broken his legs. That is all I know."

Shortly thereafter, the government forcibly removed all the able-bodied men from the village, as the country had gone to war. The old man's son, however, was spared since his legs were broken.

Good luck, bad luck: Who can tell… and so the fable can go on perpetually.

In our own lives we often career from one "good luck" occurrence to another "bad luck" event, blaming everything and everyone along the way. Accepting complete responsibility for everything in our life, empowers us to move beyond the blame game and our often faulty and unreliable power of perception.

Accepting Responsibility...

In summary, accepting responsibility means being prepared to do whatever it takes to get your relationship back on track.

'Accepting Responsibility' weaves inherently throughout all five drops of this formula. I'm sure you can see that it's not possible to 'Pause'- Drop One, unless you 'Accept Responsibility' for doing so.

'Reflecting'- Drop Two, also requires a good dose of responsibility… you accept responsibility when you are willing to acknowledge how it occurs for others. And as you will soon discover, the last two drops of the rescue remedy also include their fair share of the 'responsibility factor'.

Our next drop - Drop Four - 'Drop the Pain, teaches you to how to return your relationship 'back to that loving place'… the place we all hanker for.

And don't worry, if things are so tough that you have forgotten what that 'loving place' even looks like and haven't got a clue how to get back there, **Drop Four** will show you just how easy it is to move beyond the pain of conflict.

Key Points from Chapter Three - Drop the Blame (Accept Responsibility)

- **Take 100% responsibility for everything in your life.** When you do this you automatically give up the 'victim mentality' and take back your power. Remember, if it's all the other person's fault, there is very little chance of resolution. So take responsibility to work through to the other side of your conflicts by using the Five Drops.

- **Discover your own contribution to the problem.** This takes courage and humility. Remember, the only person you can truly change is yourself. Look for the kernel of truth that you need to take responsibility for and ask your spouse for more information without getting defensive.

- **The Mind - don't be fooled by the 'meaning machine'.** We give meaning to every event in our life and often our meaning is distorted. Many of our '*mis*-understandings' are exactly that...we fail to really understand. That's where reflection comes in. Be responsible and take the time to find out what is really going on.

- **Responsibility - it weaves through all five drops.** It's everywhere! If you have made it this far in the Five Drop process, you have already shown commitment as well as a deep sense of responsibility. You are refusing to act out the victim role or come across as a 10 year old having a temper tantrum. You have come a long way!

CHAPTER 4

Drop the Pain (Reconnect with Your Higher Self)

In Drops One and Two we were battling to overcome the modes of ignorance and passion. In those drops we learned the importance of *'keeping a cool head'* and *'seeing another's perspective'*. In Drop Three goodness became prominent as we chose to stop blaming others and *'accepted responsibility'* for everything in our lives... the good, the bad and the ugly.

Now in Drop Four we move forward to *'re-align ourselves with our highest intentions'* and to clear out any obstacles that may still be loitering in our path.

But... before we get started!

I feel compelled at this point to share one of my deepest realizations about working with the Five Drop Formula. It's so important that I've got to shout it out, loud and clear... **Don't Skim Over Drop Two - Reflection!** Yes, getting into reflection has to be the single-most important ingredient for turning around any conflict. If you skimmed over this drop and didn't really get there, you may find you have to revisit it until you do.

My husband and I have found that sometimes we have to revisit Drop Two a few times in the process of working to the other side of any conflict. You will know if you need to revert back to *'reflecting'* when there is still a lot of anger or frustration surrounding your issue. It's hard to move on to the next steps until you have understood how it is for the other person; this means getting into their shoes and really feeling how it is for them.

Once Drop Two *'Reflection'* is fully accomplished you should feel a surge of optimism at the possibility of successfully working through your upset. Drop Three *'Accepting Responsibility'* also soothes and heals your conflict because it reassures both parties of seeing it through to the end. This inspires confidence in a mood of total commitment. Drop Three then glides perfectly into Drop Four, where you get to let go of all your hurt and resentment and realign yourself and your relationship back to where you want it to be.

So What is a 'Reconnect'?

Simply stated, *'reconnect'* means to realign ourselves back to where we want to be in our life. Let's call it our higher self or best self. In the relationship context, we often refer to it as getting back to that *'loving place'*. Unfortunately for many people, that loving place may seem like light years away. This is because their relationship has become undermined by one of the biggest and most insidious pitfalls that can besiege any healthy relationship; unresolved issues... or as we prefer to call it 'stuff under the rug'.

Stuff Under the Rug

Once we were counselling a couple in conflict. We had worked through the first three drops...:'Pausing', 'Reflecting' and 'Accepting Responsibility'. They got that part easily. However, when we got to the concept of returning back to that loving place in the relationship, the wife began to look doubtful. "Well, I can't even remember that loving place...it was so long ago". Her husband agreed adding, "Yeah, loving place...what does that look like? We just have so much resentment between us." This kind of response clearly indicates that the couple have amassed many unresolved issues.

When you lack effective tools or strategies to deal with the constant stream of issues that surface in your relationship, the predictable default is to sweep them 'under the rug' where they begin to pile up; hidden but not cleared.

Stuff under the rug is treacherous - you can pretend that it has 'gone away' or that it's not really important, but it's simply amassing until one day the slightest issue trips you up and sparks a huge volcanic eruption. You scratch your head in bewilderment. "How could such a small thing cause such a huge explosion?" But remember... it **isn't** the small issues that cause the BIG reaction; it's the accumulated pile of unresolved issues that has led to such a hair trigger reaction.

Years ago a close friend of mine shared that one day she made a casual comment which she considered, in her own words, as 'not so earth-shattering'. The reaction; her calm and mellow husband picked up an object and hurled it at the wall. My friend was shocked at the raw anger of her husband as well as the gaping hole in the wall. "What did I say that was so bad?" she asked. I knew her husband, normally a quiet and patient man who wouldn't hurt a fly. It was glaringly apparent to me that this couple had amassed a mountain of 'stuff under the rug' for her husband to have reacted so explosively.

In Denial

Our unaddressed issues can develop into patterns that eat away at the very fibre of relationships. All those seemingly minor ripples; those gnarly little issues that we face every day; can over time build into patterns of resentment. We think we are doing a great job when we smooth them over. Some of us even live in a selfish land of denial, where we choose to disconnect altogether from any issue that might come up.

It's not MY problem!

A wife who had only been married for a couple of years was lamenting that the 'bliss period' of her marriage had already ended. "We used to be so happy and now we are often so angry at each other." When I probed a little further I could immediately detect the many repressed issues that this couple were reluctant to address. In this case the husband was more in a denial mode. *"I have no problem with anything,"* he would say. *"It's just her... she has problems. No problems from my side. I'm fine!"*

Hmmm... this doesn't even make sense does it? It is hardly ever one person's problem in relationship issues. We learnt that in Drop Two; Drop the Vain.

Besides, if your spouse has problems in your relationship; you **do** have problems whether you like it or not! You wouldn't have to be an expert astrologer to know where this relationship could end up if they continue repressing and stuffing their issues under the rug.

Why Am I So Angry!

Acknowledging the existence of all your *'unresolved conflicts'* gives you the answer as to why you feel such resentment, frustration and anger towards your husband/wife. This is important! Over time you have created these unhealthy behaviours, which have morphed into patterns.

The difference now is that when they come up, you **will** be equipped to effectively deal with them. Now instead of focusing on what went wrong, you will have an effective set of tools and strategies that will enable you to diffuse the heat of an upset. This takes away the fear and helplessness and empowers you to keep your relationship clear and uncluttered.

What's Your Style ?

There are a myriad ways and styles of sweeping your stuff under the rug. See if you can recognise any of these;

1. Avoidance: We just pretend nothing happened - we grin and bear it with a smile. Some of us don't even bother with the grin. We scowl and sulk and purse our lips - but still manage to shove it all under the rug. Actually we don't want to touch the problem because we are too scared of it escalating into conflict. We have been there before and it wasn't pretty.

It's not hard to see that such couples often drift apart due to a lack of authentic communication. Couples using this type of avoidance technique don't have effective ways to deal with conflict and they know it.

This was my style. My husband used to call me *'the rock'* when I went into this mode. Avoidance conversations usually went something like this.

"Is anything wrong? Have I done something to upset you?"

"No... nothing's wrong. I'm fine."

"But you look a bit upset. I can feel something's not right."

"No." (forced smile) "I'm fine... really I'm fine!"

This avoidance dialogue reminds me of the *'tongue in cheek'* advice to the male species called; *'Five Deadly Terms used by a Woman'*. The vocabulary list below is floating around the Internet with all sorts of variations, so we can't give it proper credit. However it is amusing, relevant and I for one can relate to it!

When a woman says...

FINE...

It is not fine at all. This is the word women use to end an argument when **they** are right and they think **you** need to 'zip it'.

NOTHING...

The calm before the storm. This means **something**, and you **should** be worried. Arguments that begin with *'nothing'* usually end in 'fine.'

GO AHEAD...

This is a dare, not permission. Don't do it!

THAT'S OKAY...

She wants to think long and hard before deciding how and when you *will pay for your mistake.*

WHATEVER...

A woman's way of saying 'damn you'!

BONUS WORD... WOW!

Beware! This is not a compliment. She is amazed that one person could be so incredibly stupid.

When I read this I thought...hmmm...that Mars and Venus guy was right; we really are from different planets!

2. Helplessness: Here we acknowledge that there is a problem but we can't or don't want to deal with it, so we settle for an uneasy truce. We feel the strain from the conflict pattern, but with unfounded optimism we ignore it, hoping it will miraculously go away.

We have counselled couples who *live* in this place. I remember one husband expressing distantly, "She can live her life...I will live mine. We leave each other alone and don't fight anymore *(actually we hardly even talk anymore)* but we 'stay' together for the sake of the children." Sounds noble, and the part about staying together deserves acknowledgement; but this type of relationship often disintegrates into resentment. Besides, do we really need to settle for this?

3. Competition: I win, you lose. Might is right. Someone wins through aggression or argumentative force - someone loses (if even just to 'keep the peace'). The loser usually becomes the proverbial martyr.

Unless we are genuinely *'more tolerant than a tree'* this unexpressed resentment builds up and results in a relationship that is constantly tense. This situation is ripe for 'volcanic explosions'.

I saw my parents play this one out and it was not nice. My mother took the role of the martyr while it seemed that my father always 'won'. *'Don't get dad mad'* was my mother's way of coping or 'keeping the peace' as she termed it. But our home was never peaceful. We could all feel the tension as soon as we walked through the door. This piled up resentment was tangible and seemed to constantly permeate the ether in our home. It killed my parents' marriage even though they physically *'stayed together'* until we had all flown the nest.

4. Compromise: This one *sounds* healthy and on the whole, it is generally a less volatile option. It even appears on the surface like a possible Win/Win solution. But in reality the outcome is still predominantly Lose/Lose. We compromise to keep the peace, but are both secretly unsatisfied with the outcome. Still, we push on and end up settling for less. If the compromise is more on the Lose/Lose side it generally doesn't last, as no one can keep it up for too long. This builds up resentment and frustration and even more stuff gets swept under the rug.

Counselling... Your Day in Court

"Coming together is a beginning; keeping together is progress; working together is success."

– HENRY FORD

A professional Christian counsellor I once met shared the following with me...

"In my 20 years of experience counselling couples there are two things I never assume about both partners;

1) *that they are willing and able to see their contribution to problems and*

2) *that they have the emotional clarity to communicate objectively."*

Couples who have opted for counselling are always eager and ready to talk about their problems. Finally, they have someone to listen to them. They want it all out in the open...'warts and all'. They freely bring up past difficulties. And what they especially crave is for someone to help them prove who was right and who was wrong.

However, despite having surrendered to a counselling process, many couples are still so volatile and desperate to be heard, that they willingly use the counselling session itself as a blaming and shaming venue.

When we observe that couples have entered this 'red hot conflict zone' it clearly indicates that they have accumulated so much *stuff under the rug*' that it has finally reached eruption point.

Drum Roll...The Good News

The impressive thing with the Five Drop Formula is that you don't have to dredge up all your past issues and attempt to fix them as many traditional therapists suggest. In fact when you become proficient at using this formula, you won't ever need a counsellor.

Traditional therapists often encourage you to recapture your feelings, to get in touch with your emotions and to identify all the compelling factors. They scrutinise and dissect your underlying dysfunctions.

Unfortunately, this type of therapy has the tendency to culminate in some form of the 'blame game'. It often turns into a quest to prove who was right and who was wrong, or even who was **more** right or **more** wrong (if you get what I mean). So much time and trauma is involved, what to speak of the expense. And to top it all off, statistics show that this kind of therapy is generally not very effective.

The Magic Formula... Move Beyond the Past

Forget the past that sleeps
Nor in the future dwell at all
Be with times that are with thee
And progress ye shall call.

– SRILA BHAKTIVINODE THAKUR

The mode of goodness (Sattva-guna) enters here again as a prime ingredient in this *'magic formula'* for dealing with what is happening right now in your relationship.

You got tripped up. However the conflict you are dealing with is only a temporary blip in eternity. Right now you have successfully worked together through the first three drops. You are now working in harmony. You have miraculously shifted from being upset to being calm. You have both practiced listening and have shown empathy. You have stopped blaming each other and have accepted responsibility to do whatever it takes to come to the other side of conflict. There is light at the end of the tunnel. You are now in the best possible position to *reconnect with your 'best self', your higher self; the person you truly are.*

When you keep your focus on each successful step as you work together through the 5 Drop Formula all the stuff amassed under the rug magically dissipates! You can then re-align with your positive intentions for each other, and move on towards solving the conflict at hand.

Start by celebrating and acknowledging each other for how far you have now come. (You'll learn more about how to do that in Drop 5 Pouring on the Energy)

Realise that what you have experienced is most likely a familiar conflict that has formed into a pattern over time; one that you have been unintentionally perpetuating. Feel reassured that you now have a process to deal effectively with each new issue that arises by going through the Five Drop Rescue Remedy steps.

The Five Drop Formula trains you to use the spiritual principle of focusing on the present and letting go of the past. ***Being fully present in each moment is EXTREMELY POWERFUL!***

Enter...Mindfulness

Although the popular term 'Mindfulness' sounds very Buddhist or Zen, it is the same principle Srila Prabhupada referred to as being *'conscious'*.

In reality, we have complete freedom to *consciously* choose our state at every moment and we get to write our own script every day. Conversely, we can just as easily choose a different way of being; hankering about the future or lamenting about the past. Bhagavad-gita advises us to stop this hankering and lamenting (*'na socati na kanksati'* Bhagavad-gita 18.54) and to access the mode of goodness, where we live in the present and make genuine and intentional progress.

Develop your 'Mindful' muscles

Like every other human competency, the ability to function in a mindful or conscious way is something that takes proactive cultivation and consistent practice. You don't get physically fit by sitting around waiting for it to happen. You need to take action. The more focused, precise and well-informed the action, the quicker you will get to where you want to be and the more lasting your results. It is the same with developing mindfulness. It is a muscle that needs to be toned and strengthened.

Whenever any good result surfaces in personal relationships, invariably we find that 'Mindfulness' or 'the mode of goodness' has been accessed in some way or other. Time and time again I find myself coming to the realization that everything good; every worthy deed, every positive result, every wise thought or decision I make, all spring from being able to access this 'Mindfulness' mode.

Sounds so simple doesn't it? In theory it is simple. But to rise above the modes of ignorance and passion, and make 'Mindfulness' our new default setting is no small thing.

Miracle Spray or Learned Habit?

Being able to access this 'Mindful' or 'Conscious' Mode' under all circumstances is more about *'the development of a learned habit'* than some 'miracle spray' we pull out of our pocket. It often begins with realisation born from experiences that teach, inspire and drive us into action. We learn valuable life lessons through both pain and joy. In our conditioned state we often choose to learn from suffering. Realising that whenever we succumb to the lower modes we inevitably end up in ignorance and distress is a vitally important component to conquering our negative patterns. However, acting upon this realisation and being able to access a higher state of being, requires constant practice and determination.

A few words of Caution - Don't Try and Reconnect Others!

Reconnecting is very powerful. You will find it a great tool that you can use whenever you get off track. Just like a button on your computer, press your own personal reconnect button whenever you find yourself being the person you really don't want to be; the critical, blaming, negative person you want to change. Learn to reconnect with your 'higher self'. This can develop into a wonderful, life-long habit.

However, there is a warning here. Do not try to 'reconnect' others. We can only 'reconnect' ourselves. When we try to force others to reconnect, they get the clear message that we are trying to fix or control them. This never works and it usually invokes the old attack/defend response.

Just imagine how this would go down...

"Prabhu, you know you over-reacted there. I think you really need to 'reconnect'."

versus...

*"OK, so now that I realise and understand where you are coming from (Drop Two – Reflection). I think **I need to 'reconnect'** and then we can work together to solve the problem."*

Just as in Drop Two - Drop the Vain... when we reflect on how it is for others, it inspires and encourages them to do the same. Similarly when you reconnect with your higher self and get back on track, others feel safe and inspired to do likewise.

Enter...The Third Alternative

Because you have used 'reflection' and 'empathy', and you're well on your way to re-aligning with your higher self, you are now in the best position and consciousness to work through the problem with what Srila Prabhupada termed a 'cool head'. Now that you both refuse to play the *blame game,* the time is ripe to put your heads together and come up with a solution; one that works for you both!

Steven Covey talks about solving problems using a brilliant concept called "The Third Alternative". In any conflict, the First Alternative is my way, and the Second Alternative is usually your way. The fight then boils down to a question of whose way is better. The Third Alternative moves beyond your way or my way to a higher and better way - one that allows both parties to emerge from even the most turbulent of conflicts in a far better place than either had envisioned.

The beauty of the Third Alternative is that nobody has to give up anything, and everyone wins. This allows you to build strong relationships, still recognising your diverse needs and wants. It's born from the attitude of winning together.

This means that instead of always compromising, you intentionally work together to think up something that works really well for you both. It's about realising you don't always have to settle for less when you are problem solving. I love the Third Alternative concept. It is so satisfying when you come up with creative solutions. It gets you out of that stagnated 'my way' or 'your way' place. You begin to realise that when you put your heads together you can always come up with a 'Third Alternative' that works beautifully for you both. Here is a typical everyday type of experience that illustrates how we have used the Third Alternative.

Our 'Broc Bin' Problem

We all have a cooking day in our extended family situation. We call our kitchen organic scrap bin the *'broc bin'*. This was named by my husband's 95 year old Scottish mother. I think it may be short for 'broccoli'; not sure but that's what she called it and it just stuck. We decided that emptying the 'broc bin' daily would work if we did it on our individual cooking days. Our broc bin is emptied into a large compost bin which lies about 20 metres from the house. This system worked well for a while until one day while I was emptying the 'broc bin', a huge rat jumped out from the compost and lunged straight at me.

That was it for me...I just stopped emptying it on my day; hoping that no-one would notice. My husband (who never misses a trick) *did* notice. I explained to him about the enormous rat (whose size magically increased every time I talked about it). My husband knows me well; he did not even attempt to convince me to 'get over' my rodent phobia. (I suppose you could say that he empathized with my problem... Drop Two - Reflection.) We brainstormed for a while and decided to work on a Third Alternative. We came up with the idea that if I would dry more dishes (his job), he would empty the bin on my cooking day. We were both more than satisfied with the solution. This is how easy it is. Problem.....discuss alternatives... come up with something that suits you both. End of problem!!!!

As you may have probably discerned, you don't have to be in conflict to use the Third Alternative strategy. It is a fantastic way of solving problems before they veer into conflict by creatively and proactively coming up with solutions that suit both parties. We are amazed at how quickly we can come up with a solution that suits us both. As you become skilled in using all Five Drops of the Relationship Rescue Remedy Formula, coming up with your own creative 'alternative solutions' will also become easier and easier.

A word of warning at this point. Make sure that it really is a 'Third Alternative' and not a compromise. You can test the strength of your Third Alternative by asking each other….*How would that work for you?*

Remember: The secret is to continue coming up with alternatives until you can totally affirm that the solution works well for both of you.

The Third Alternative and 'The Map Story'

You remember our 'map story' from chapter one. We finally laid that pattern to rest using 'The Third Alternative'. You will remember how I was the lousy navigator and my husband the tense driver needing clear directions. This was a pattern we played out over many years. It was also one we didn't want to deal with, so we continually stashed it under the rug. Well, if you have read this far, you now *know* what happens when you stash stuff under the rug, hoping that it will miraculously disappear. Think eruption. Correct. One day as we ambled down that well-trodden but rocky path, I exploded like the veritable volcano. I had a mini-tantrum and the street directory went flying into the back seat. I 'resigned' as navigator on the spot and opened up the conflict. It was actually liberating to finally confront our dysfunctional pattern. I often wonder why it took us so long!

Of course we paused. My husband stopped the car and we sat there in complete silence for about five minutes. One of us managed to reflect first, and I can't remember who that was. What I *do* remember is finally confessing to possessing very little spatial intelligence. My husband also admitted to a lack of patience when the directions were not as clear as he would have liked. Once we had empathised and accepted responsibility it was now time to work towards a Third Alternative. My husband volunteered that he would look up the directions to our destination before we left. His condition was that I would let him have as much time as he needed to do this. This suits my husband's disposition as he hates being rushed. You may have already guessed that this was before GPS technology made our lives so much easier! We were both happy with our solution and it works perfectly to this day. (By the way, we still don't have a GPS).

So now you see how The Third Alternative works. Get creative and have fun with it. You will be amazed at how imaginative and innovative you can get.

Four Drops Done.... Get Ready to Dive In!

Now you have completed the first four drops of the Relationship Rescue Remedy. This is all you really need to resolve your conflicts. So what is the need for a fifth drop? This last drop, which is often neglected or minimised, has the power to rebuild damaged relationships as well as to nourish and strengthen even the best of relationships. So please dive into the **next drop** and splash it everywhere!

Key Points from Chapter Four - Drop the Pain (Reconnect with Your Higher Self)

- **Don't skim over drop Two (Reflection).** Sometimes you may have to roll back to Drop 2 (Reflection). You will know when you need to do this if you still sense some anger around your issue.

- **Reconnect - just like on your computer.** Sound's easy... it is. If you have travelled this far in the Five Drop process, this step will occur naturally ...unless of course you still have *'stuff under the rug'*.

- **Can't get back to that loving place - it could be the 'stuff under the rug'.** When couples have become practised at sweeping their issues under the rug, they may not even remember what that 'loving place' was like. There is no need to worry about this. Now you *do* have the tools to successfully work through your issues instead of repressing them. Once you become practiced at clearing your issues that loving place will re-emerge.

- **No need to dredge up the past - live in the 'now'.** The good news is that you don't need to drag all your past issues out and deal with them. Just acknowledging and recognising your dysfunctional patterns is enough. When your familiar conflict patterns attempt to rear their ugly heads and destroy the peace of your relationship you will know just what to do.

- **Don't try to reconnect others - it doesn't work.** No-one wants to be 'fixed'. We can only reconnect with ourselves, and when we do it is powerful. It's just like racing to reflection. When you reconnect with your higher self, you open the door and make it easy for others to follow.

- **The Third Alternative - a win/win solution.** You can really have fun and get creative here to think up solutions to your problems. Remember to always test your Third Alternative by checking how well this will work for *both* of you. Don't forget to use the Third Alternative proactively whenever you find yourself differing in opinion. Ask the magic question, "Is there a way we can solve this that will work really well for us both?"

CHAPTER 5

Pour On the Energy (Be the Honey Bee!)

"Among the uncommonly good souls there are still gradations, and the best good soul is one who accepts an insignificant asset of a person and magnifies that good quality."

– SRIMAD-BHAGAVATAM.4.4.12 PURPORT

At this point you have become familiar with the first 4 steps - Pause, Reflect, Accept Responsibility, and Reconnect, and should have moved to the other side of your conflict. It's now time for us to show you how to utilise those *'moments of success'* to start building an extraordinary relationship.

Drop Five of the Rescue Remedy: 'Pour on the Energy', calls not for drops, but mega doses; poured on! Apply liberally and consistently and watch the health and vitality of your relationships soar. This final step has both healing and transformational properties that not only complete the conflict resolution, but also stand alone as a daily practice that will change your whole life. As a *reactive* formula this last drop has the power to minimise and dismantle conflict situations and as a *proactive* formula it both deepens and strengthens your relationships.

Time to Celebrate!

We are often unaware or unconscious of our progress. This is frequently true in the context of devotional service itself. Like me, you probably shudder to think what you would be doing now if it wasn't for the mercy of the pure devotee. I know for certain that I would be existing in a state of 'not so blissful ignorance'; suspended between hankering for what I want, lamenting for what I have lost, and wondering why my life was not turning out like the romance novels I devoured in my youth.

When you have made your way through the first four drops, however imperfectly: it really is time to celebrate. Reflect upon the following for a moment... Isn't it a fact that every time you *'paused'*, you gained a victory over your enemy; anger? Isn't it also true that every time you attempted to *'reflect and empathise'*, you crushed your false ego and fed your authentic ego? When you *'accepted responsibility'* to do whatever it took to work through a conflict, you displayed great commitment, maturity and strength. *'Reconnecting'* with your higher yourself, and working cooperatively to come up with new alternatives to solve your problems, indicated your creativity and intelligence. Are you getting the picture? Success breeds success. By energising your successes you will get more of them!

Pour it On!

Instead of waiting around for the next inevitable upset, take every opportunity to build upon the moments of success you have already experienced while you have been working together through your issues. 'Pouring on the energy' involves acknowledging and energising each other for all the great qualities you have both displayed in the process.

Unfortunately, this simple but revolutionary concept 'runs against the grain' and collides with our general tendency of minimising or dismissing those important victories; those defining moments of success.

Instead, our 'negative default setting' kicks in and drives us to focus on what's lacking. We hanker and lament for what is lacking now; all that has lacked in the past and worry about how the future may continue to lack! This attitude cultivates negativity and only perpetuates the cycle of conflict and frustration.

'Pouring on the energy' focuses on success; on taking those seemingly insignificant molecules of success and magnifying them.

Here's how it works and it's very simple. After you have completed the first four drops and have dissipated your conflicts, take the time and energy to acknowledge each other.

It could sound something like this:

"Thanks for sticking with the process and understanding where I was coming from. I know it was hard for you, but you really got into 'my shoes' and saw how it was happening for me. This means so much to me."

Get the idea. The more genuine, heart-felt and specific the better!

Why We Fear Encouraging Others...

"In marriage, let each partner be an encourager rather than a critic; a forgiver rather than a collector of hurts; an enabler rather than a reformer."

– H. NORMAN WRIGHT

As devotees, we are naturally wary of giving and receiving (false) praise. We worry and fret about 'puffing up' each other's false egos. However, although this can be a genuine concern, such a mentality leads us into a type of 'scarcity consciousness'. This can adversely affect the very depth of our relationships making them impersonal and dry.

It goes without saying that in the materialistic context, false flattery and praise does happen. People **do** praise each other with ulterior motives; to manipulate and exploit for gaining sense gratification. We rightly fear this. Notwithstanding, when we neglect opportunities for encouraging others, we miss out on the true value of using such appreciation to inspire others to live up to their true potential.

Scarcity Mentality and Impersonalism

I have often mused that we have a similarly dysfunctional mentality around the power of prayer. I was brought up as a *'good catholic'*. We prayed for anything and everything *'under the sun'*. God was indeed our 'order supplier'. From a top grade at school to a new bike, I prayed for things I needed or wanted. My mother prayed constantly for our material success and our safety, so I had a good role model. When I became a devotee I was suddenly confronted with the selfish nature of my prayer habits. I realised I had been asking God to serve **me**. This prompted a huge paradigm shift. I began to take pleasure in serving God and trusting that He would always take care of me. However, I simultaneously threw out all personal prayer in the process; *the proverbial baby with the bathwater*. It took me years to get in touch with any form of personal prayer again.

We may have a similar misconception around actively encouraging others or ourselves. We are worried about building up false egos. If your praise is false, empty or manipulative, you **do** need to be concerned. But, just as there is genuine healthy prayer in our Vaisnava tradition, there are also a myriad of healthy ways of encouraging ourselves and others that will feed our motivation and inspire bhakti. And let's face it - unless we have attained the stage of pure unalloyed devotion, we all want and **need** this kind of positive encouragement and feedback to grow in our devotional service.

Radhanath Swami relates an experience that illustrates this fear of praise mentality perfectly.

> *I once told an ashram leader that one of his mentees was a great singer, and I just love the prayer chants he leads in the morning. As I expressed heart-felt appreciation for his student's musical talents, I saw the leader alarmed. "Never tell him he's a good singer", he gravely expressed concern, "he needs to be humble, and if you speak all good things about him, he'll be spoiled and may get puffed up." I reasoned, "But how will he feel encouraged?" to which the leader snubbed me; "you don't worry about that. These boys need to be tough and disciplined, not pampered and spoiled with praise." I protested, "I agree we shouldn't flatter them but there are certainly ways of encouraging positively. While urging him to be prayerful and humble, we can also appreciate his devotional singing and these kind words will go a long way and help him sustain his other services."*

> *I told my ashram friend that as a guide he may also alienate his students if he withholds honest appreciation and only admonishes them. I helped him envision a future scenario where we lose this talented member because no one encourages him here. He may either leave or go away to another ashram with bitterness in his heart. Do we really want that? My concerns seemed to make sense to my friend; he trusted me and soon rectified his relationship with his counselee. Let's not be miserly; shower appreciation when it's due and encourage all.*

When we see others who are gifted and talented we naturally want them to use these gifts in devotional service. Many individuals are unaware of their true potential and a few genuine words of encouragement by others can make a huge difference in their spiritual journey.

You Can Choose!

There may be a need to stress once more that having a successful relationship doesn't mean that there will never be any conflict. Srila Prabhupada told us to forget **utopia!** He urged his householder disciples to live together peacefully and happily, but he warned us that there will always be waves in the material ocean.

The golden rule to remember… and this one needs drumming into our heads.

It's not conflict that damages relationships. It's how we choose to respond to our conflicts… with 'choose' being the operative word.

Abandoning our Fly Mentality

"Srila Prabhupada would see the spark of any sincerity in a person's heart and dismiss all of his other bad qualities and just try to fan and kindle that spark into becoming the fire of love of god."

– RADHANATH SWAMI VYASA PUJA LECTURE 2010

The energy principle is strikingly simple. Whatever we give our energy to, we get more of … and that's it! Start giving your energy to even the smallest measure of success, then fan that spark and you will get more of the same.

To achieve this we have to abandon our stubborn *'fly'* mentality. Even when entering a beautiful and fragrant flower garden, the fly will search out something rotten. He will continually buzz around thinking, 'I must seek out the stool, it must be here somewhere; if I look hard enough I know I can find it'. Whatever the situation, no matter how bright, clean and pure, the fly can't shake off his *'stool finding'* mentality. How many of us resemble that fly and how damaging can this attitude be to our relationships and our spiritual lives? Our Vaisnava literature is brimming with warnings to be careful of offences against devotees. But often we forget that those 'nearest and dearest' to us are included in this warning. We may bow and scrape, showing the greatest respect to senior Vaisnavas, Sannyasis and Gurus, but at the very same time treat our family members or other *ordinary devotees* with either careless familiarity or outright contempt.

The Christian monk Thomas A Kempis warns about this criticising mentality in the thirteenth-century work *Imitation of Christ* and urges us to look inward.

Try to bear patiently with the defects and infirmities of others, whatever they may be, because you also have many a fault which others must endure. If you cannot make yourself what you wish to be, how can you bend others to your will? We want them to be perfect, yet we do not correct our own faults. We wish them to be severely corrected, yet we will not correct ourselves.

Honey Bee Training

"A devotee never finds fault with others, but tries to find his own and thus rectify them as far as possible."

– SRIMAD-BHAGAVATAM, 1.13.33 PURPORT

Are you ready to cast off your old 'fly body' and get into training to become the "Honey Bee" you really are. Srila Prabhupada repeatedly requested his followers to imbibe this key Vaisnava principle.

Tamal Krishna Maharaja relates an example when urging his own disciples to see the good in each other and work in harmony.

> *What is Krishna trying to teach us? He is trying to teach us that each of us should just learn to get along. So many times I saw examples. Prabhupada would have to settle disputes between devotees; many, many times. We had one example, I had this treasurer, you*

know, a very difficult person. This person would take all the sankir-tana money, and immediately after getting the money, he would close the treasury. We couldn't get any money for buying food, or for buying the deities things. And when the weekends would come he would immediately disappear. So there was no money. I had practically pulled out my sikha. There was just so much frustration, because I was in charge of the temple.

Finally I went to Prabhupada and said, "This is impossible. This person is really impossible." Prabhupada said, "What is his crime?" I said, "His crime is that as soon as he gets all the collection, he closes the treasury. And on the weekends he disappears." Prabhupada said, "Very good treasurer! Very good treasurer!" He said, "The first qualification of a good treasurer, he doesn't like to spend money." And I said, "So, that's the end of my complaint."

Tamal Krishna Maharaja ended this recount by succinctly summing up the difference between criticism and what he alternatively termed, 'positive criticism'.

> *'Positive criticism is when you have no malice in your heart, when you try to correct a person. When there is not the slightest malice in your heart, that's positive criticism.'*

The key to constructive criticism (and there **is** a time and place for it) is to have no malice in your heart. Too often we are **pots calling kettles black** with varying degrees of the malice factor, and our recipient definitely feels the weight of our intentions.

Of course there is, and always will be, a time and a place for a 'tough love' approach. Think about Vidura urging Dhritarastra to retire to the forest and stop relying on the mercy of the Pandavas. Vidura chastises his brother with harsh words and it works. There was no malice in the heart of Vidura; only love and concern for his elder brother and this is the defining principle. No matter how strong our words, if our intention springs from a place of love the recipient will feel it.

When Your Best Lecture Just Doesn't Work

"Men marry women with the hope they will never change. Women marry men with the hope they will change. Invariably they are both disappointed."

– ALBERT EINSTEIN

Sometimes we itch to give the perfect lecture to our spouse, kids and whoever else we would dearly love to *'fix'*. I speak from realisation as I have been there a thousand times! It's not that we should never be able to guide and counsel others. But if your best lectures, dripping with profound wisdom, are not working and end up as just another ingredient of the conflict soup, you may need to examine your heart, and reconsider how best to demonstrate your love.

When Srila Prabhupada *'gave the sauce'* as we used to call it, he knew the recipient could generally take it because there was no material motive behind the apparent criticism; only love and concern. Conversely, when we try to imitate this *'giving of the sauce'* it often seems to backfire drastically. Srutakirti dasa relates that when he was Srila Prabhupada's servant, Srila Prabhupada rarely chastised him, knowing how sensitive he was; sensing that he would not be able to take it. I would hazard to guess that our motives for correcting others are more often than not of the mixed variety and we therefore end up with less than desirable results.

Start Building Miracles from Molecules

"Everyone should be friendly for the service of the Lord. Everyone should praise another's service to the Lord and not be proud of his own service. This is the way of Vaisnava thinking, Vaikuntha thinking."

–SRIMAD-BHAGAVATAM 7.5.12 PURPORT

When you practice the habit of energizing success in others, even if it appears that you have very little to build upon, you take your relationship to a higher level. Instead of searching for faults and focusing on failures, practice building upon even the smallest whiff of success.

When you think about it, this is how it probably was at the beginning of your relationship. You donned your blinkers, put on your rose coloured glasses, and saw all the wonderful things about your spouse. Looking for 'faults' just wasn't on the menu. Intuitively you knew this would have been counterproductive to developing a healthy relationship.

In retrospect you could argue, *"Back in the day when we were basking in the throes of early love we must have been a little deluded or imbalanced. But now that I know what he/she is **really** like I have woken up."*

To what extent this **reasoning** holds true is hard to say. But one thing you can know for sure is that your focus has definitely changed; you are now acutely aware of, or even searching for faults. Sadly, if you continue down this track your relationship will reflect more of what you don't want… faults and problems!

Getting Back on Track

I remember one devotee relating to my husband that his wife had dramatically changed since their marriage. "She is not the same girl I married", he complained. "When we were first married, she used to speak to me so sweetly, now she snaps at me most of the time." My husband listened to the devotee and then gently asked him if his wife had any good qualities, to which he nodded. My husband then requested him to write down all the positive things he could think of about his wife. This devotee soon came up with a substantial list which included things like;

She listens to my problems and my dreams

She cleans our house

She is super organised

She laughs at my jokes

She puts up with my mess

She encourages me in my spiritual life

"Hmmm, perhaps you could start giving energy to some of the positive things she is already doing", my husband suggested. The young husband looked thoughtful. "Yes, you are right, I never really show my appreciation for what she does. I guess I thought that by pointing out what she could be doing better, I was helping her." He then agreed to focus on and acknowledge all the wonderful things his wife was already doing. A few weeks later he reported the results. "At first she was quite suspicious, but after a while when she saw and felt my sincerity, she began to accept my acknowledgements and now our relationship is back on track."

Morphing Takes Time

Be warned; transforming from a fly into a *'honey bee'* takes conscious and consistent effort. At first we may keep slipping back to our fly setting, but don't get discouraged. It's like anything you try to change; it takes time and persistent effort. So don't sit around waiting for your next upset or misunderstanding before trying this out. Start immediately to re-channel your tendency from *'energising the negativity'* in your relationships to 'energising those special moments of success'... however small! Holding this new mindset generates a positive force that will deepen and strengthen the very foundation of your relationship.

A Serious Honey Bee- Jayananda Dasa

"So in your letter you are not finding fault with anyone. So you are good Vaishnava. You do not find fault with anyone. This is the qualification. We should always think ourselves humble and meek. This you must know. So we all have to cooperate amongst ourselves, otherwise what will people think if we ourselves fight with one another? A devotee is always ideal in behavior."

– SRILA PRABHUPADA LETTER 1974

Talking of the 'honey bee' mentality- our very own Jayananda dasa lived his life in this state. One of my favourite recounts is what I call, 'The Fish Seller Story'. The setting was San Francisco where Jayananda would regularly lead devotees in kirtan down by the wharf. The fish vendors on the wharf were not happy with the devotees invading their domain. To irritate the devotees they would throw stinky fish water on their path just as they arrived. This intentional insult made many of the devotees angry. But Jayananda accessed his 'honey bee' attitude to defuse this potentially explosive situation. He asked some devotees to bake cookies and smilingly presented them to the fish vendors, thanking them for always cleaning the path for the devotees to dance on. His warmth and humour melted the hard hearts of those fish vendors. They stopped throwing the water and began smiling and waving whenever the devotees danced by.

Start Small

Here are some important points to remember when encouraging and energising others. It's about shining a light and reflecting back to the other person what attributes you perceive in the form of authentic appreciations. What we are looking for are those *'moments of success'* displayed by the other person. This is where we remind ourselves to be like honeybees. Reflect this back to the other person with sincere words of recognition and acknowledgement.

Please don't wait for your spouse to change dramatically or to display complete consistency in any desired behaviour. You will be missing many great opportunities if you do this. One woman voiced how she didn't feel authentic encouraging all the small endeavours her husband was making to become a better listener. *"OK, so he listened to me without interrupting once. But that hardly ever happens!"* Who does that sound like... the Honey Bee or the Fly?

The secret is to acknowledge all positive shifts, however slight. Remember, it's the molecules we are looking for. Start with what you see and build upon it.

Be Specific

It is crucial to be specific when you energise the positive qualities you see in others. "Well done", "Good job" etc. sound nice but they are vague, sparse and really don't tell us very much. The more specific the better!

Here are some examples of getting specific:

"The way you managed to give me the time to explain myself was truly amazing. You gave me all the time I needed to get across my feelings and explain why I was upset. Your patience and understanding are awesome."

"When you reflected back to me, how you could understand why I could easily be disappointed with you, it made such a difference. That helped me to open up to seeing how it was for you. You have the power of deep reflection and humility."

When I first began my honey bee training, I feared sounding fake and 'cheesy'. Describing others' good qualities did not seem to come naturally, as I struggled to come up with suitable adjectives in various contexts. But after a while of practice, it began to flow more naturally and genuinely. As an added bonus, I discovered along the way that when you nourish others you also feel nourished.

Can you imagine a relationship, a family or a society that worked like this? Where everyone was like a honey bee buzzing around looking for nectar. It sounds 'pollyannic' (yes there is such a word; I looked it up!) but it is possible and it is within our grasp. This could be your personal default setting; your new way of being.

In my classroom practice when I first began using this principle of energising children's success, it was definitely a struggle. Sometimes I felt I was scraping the bottom of the barrel to acknowledge positive behaviours in some of my more difficult students. But I persisted, dreaming that one fine day if I kept practicing this 'honey bee mentality' it would actually become part of 'me'. It did take time, like any new skill, but I can honestly say I have permanently changed my default setting. Now, when I slip back into energising children's negative behaviour, it doesn't sit right with me. I reflect, reconnect with my higher self and get quickly back on track.

Becoming The Change!

We all want 'instant' change, but 'real' change doesn't work like that; it takes persistence, patience and determination, which are all qualities of the mode of goodness. When you change, there are clear stages you progress through. Below I have outlined the Stages of Competence we go through when we choose to learn new skills or habits. Understanding these stages will help you to see the natural phases that we go through when attempting any behaviour change.

Whenever I try to acquire a new skill or habit I am reminded of these progressive stages of competence. By acknowledging these stages – especially the one you are in – you can assure yourself of further progress. Initially described as "Four Stages for Learning Any New Skill", this theory was developed at Gordon Training International by its employee Noel Burch in the 1970s.

Stages of Competence

Stage 1: Unconsciously Incompetent

"I don't know what I don't know."

This first stage of acquiring a new skill is when you are muddling along the best you can but are unaware that you are making mistakes. This is similar to *'ignorance is bliss'*. When you get to the place of acknowledging your mistakes you pave the way for the second stage of competence. It's not until you get to the … *'hey, this is not working- in fact it has never worked'* realisation (as in our map problem scenario) that you are ready to progress to the next stage.

Stage 2: Consciously Incompetent

"I know what I don't know."

The second stage of proficiency, the phase of conscious incompetence starts when you develop awareness about the things you do not know. In this state, you plant yourself with hopes and aspirations. This stage can also be a little frustrating because you are now aware of your level of incompetence. When you first start applying the drops, you will feel something like this. *'Hmmm, what was that second drop that I was sup-posed to do... and I can never remember the third one... something about blame? Will I ever get this stuff right?'* Trust me... you just need to hang in here. It will feel a tad awkward, but with practice it will get better... and better... and even better.

Stage 3: Consciously Competent

"I grow and know and it starts to show."

A consciously competent individual dedicates himself to the improve-ment of the skill by undertaking repeated and consistent practice.

This is when you still have to think about applying the stages – it is not yet automatic or unconscious, but you are becoming competent and therefore more confident in your application and best of all - you are getting great results. This keeps you motivated and propels you into the next stage.

Stage 4: Unconsciously Competent or Mastery

"I simply go because of what I know."

As you build experience and expertise, you reach the stage of uncon-scious competence – where you hardly even have to think about the activity you have mastered.

The journey from conscious competence to unconscious competence happens quickly if constant practice is applied. However, one can still find oneself sliding in and out of unconscious competence, as one pro-gresses towards mastery. When mastery is achieved, you will dance gracefully through the five steps and easily resolve your conflicts, with-out having to think too much about it. You will instinctively know when you have not reflected enough and need to roll back to get into a deeper state of empathy. It will also become second nature to energise and encourage each other. You may still have the occasional slip-up from time to time, but you quickly get back on track, because you just don't feel right in any other state.

Your New Default Setting!

When using the 5 Drop Formula feels completely natural to you and you wonder how you ever functioned previously, you have reached unconscious competence. You are totally familiar with each drop and know all the pitfalls involved. At this stage you can dance between the drops and revisit any of them when needed.

Key Points from Chapter five - Pour on the Energy (Appreciate and Encourage)

- **Celebrate!** You've paused, reflected, accepted responsibility and returned to that loving place. If you have come this far in the process you should pat yourselves on the back and celebrate. You have come a long way...so break out the mango lassi or something!

- **Pour it on** - Appreciate and acknowledge each other for how far you've come. This may sound a little artificial or 'cheesy' at first...but once you get used to it you will be amazed at the power a few words of appreciation and encouragement can have on a relationship. Don't be a miser...pour it on!

- **Get rid of your fly mentality - become a honey bee** - We often don't realise how potently our 'fly mentality' pervades and affects our relationships. The first step is awareness and the next step is to practice your new honey-bee mentality. If you do these two things - one day you will really *be* the honey-bee!

- **Start small - build those miracles from molecules.** We often want to wait until our spouse 'reforms' into that perfect husband or wife to dish out any appreciation or acknowledgement. If you wait for that to happen you will possibly miss out on many lost opportunities. We sometimes fear that if we acknowledge those small changes... that's all we will get-*small changes*. It doesn't work like that. Magnify and energise your spouse for their slightest effort in the right direction and you will be amazed at the accumulated results.

- **It takes practice - the Stages of Competence.** Understanding the Stages of Competence and recognising where you stand in the spectrum, gives you the motivation and confidence to continue practising the Five Drops until it becomes automatic. So don't worry if it doesn't come naturally at first. Keep practicing and you will soon be dancing through the drops!

RELATIONSHIP RESCUE REMEDY FAQS

Drop 1 - Pause - Drop the Flame

Q. What if I'm way too angry to try anything?

Sometimes we are not ready to deal with an issue and just need more time to cool off. Go back and read Chapter 1 and go over all the ways described in dropping the flame to see which ones resonate with you. What works for you in one instance may not the next. Feel free to experiment with this one. Your anger could also indicate that you have unaddressed issues under that old rug, which have led to a buildup of resentment and repressed anger. It's a huge relief when we acknowledge our stuff under the rug. Remember, you don't have to drag them out and fix each one, but you do have to make a fresh start, recognise your conflict patterns and use the five drops next time an issue arises.

Drop 2 - Reflect - Drop the Vain

Q. What if I can't get to the place where I'm able to see the other person's point of view?

Yes…I have been there and have found that it usually means a longer pause time is needed. Being able to reflect effectively is also a skill that needs to be practiced. It ultimately requires us to develop some effective listening skills as well as a dash of humility which is never a bad thing. And remember the golden rule; 'he or she who gets into reflection first is never the loser'.

Drop 3 - Accept Responsibility - Drop the Blame

Q. What if it is so clear that it is his/her fault?

Have you ever had the crystal clear realisation that it really *is* the other person's fault? You are not alone… and who really knows… you may well be right. But a better question to ask is- how has that worked for you in the past? What happened when you enlightened your husband or wife with the indisputable fact that they were wholly to blame and just needed to admit it? Did they smile, agree, fall at your feet and beg for forgiveness. In your dreams!

Remember dropping the blame is not about finding out who was right or wrong, or even who was more right or wrong. It is about *you* taking responsibility to see the conflict through. Even if you are sure that it is not your fault, be assured that the other party has an equally justifiable view of the event. Everyone has their story about what happened. By trying to understand where they were coming from, without malice or judgement, you will allow them to drop their defences and assume their part in the responsibility factor.

Q. What if I accept full responsibility and the other person doesn't seem to reciprocate… i.e. they agree that I should assume responsibility for the upset?

This is our fear speaking. Again, it's not about apportioning blame. When we talk of accepting responsibility, it's not about accepting guilt for the issue at hand but about taking responsibility to work your way through the issue using the five drops, i.e. remaining calm, seeing the other's perspective etc.

Our fear warns us that the other person may not reciprocate. However I have never seen this happen. One thing to keep in mind, however, is that you must learn to detach yourself from expecting such reciprocation.

When we hold this expectation, that if I assume responsibility first, then they should immediately follow... the other person may sense this expectation and feel manipulated and refuse to reciprocate. If this happens they may be even be subconsciously testing you to see if you really mean it. Once they are satisfied, it will be easy for them to also take responsibility.

Drop 4 - Reconnect - Drop the Pain

Q. We have so much 'stuff under the rug' we can't go forward to 'that loving place'... or go back for that matter.

You have accumulated so much stuff under the rug because you didn't know how to deal with your conflicts. Now you do. Each time you effectively deal with the patterns that emerge you will gain confidence and be one step closer to your 'loving place'. Remember don't try and dredge up the past because frankly, you won't need to. All your unaddressed dysfunctional patterns will keep rearing their ugly heads until you deal with them effectively. Once you do they will be laid to rest for good (just like our map problem).

Drop 5 - Energize - Pour on the Energy

Q. Why should I energize someone for doing things that they are supposed to do, or have agreed to do?

Most of us really are misers when it comes to appreciation. We feel the need to wait for something *'big'* or totally consistent before we deem to dish out any acknowledgement or appreciation. Our logic argues that if we recognise all those small, insignificant endeavours we will never get anything more. Funny, but it doesn't work like that. When you appreciate and give your positive energy to even the smallest of things you are, in effect, depositing into your love and trust account. When you do this you get more... and ultimately much more than you ever dreamed of! Just try it and see!

THE END... AND A NEW BEGINNING!

Congratulations! You have now learned how to apply the Five Drop Rescue Remedy. We sincerely hope that you are now feeling optimistic and excited about the prospect of transforming and strengthening all your relationships.

Let this book be a guide and manual for you. Read it, highlight, share and study it together. Practice the Drops consistently... and above all don't get discouraged if you bungle it from time to time...as you most certainly will! Just keep taking the medicine... pause, reflect, accept responsibility and reconnect with who you really are! Then celebrate, acknowledge and energise your success. Follow this prescription, and repeat when needed.

WHERE TO NEXT

Chances are that if you are reading this book, you may have already completed our online training course. If not sign up for it now. Use it to consolidate and expand on what you have already learned from this short book.

http://KrishnaConsciousRelationships.com

Also please join our Facebook Group. In the group you can share your experiences and ask questions from us (Jaya Sila and Vimala) as well as the hundreds of other devotees that make up our community.

Here is the link to the group:

https://www.facebook.com/groups/relationshiprescueremedy/

If you go to Facebook and search "Relationship Rescue Remedy" the group will come up. Click on Join and we will add you to the group.

We wish you well implementing the Five Drops and look forward to meeting you either in person or in our online community.

Hare Krishna. See you there...

RECOMMENDED READINGS

Heart and Soul Connection: A Devotional Guide to Marriage Service and Love - Ghrihastha Vision Team

Experienced Grihastha devotees share skills, techniques and insights that couples can learn to have healthy marriages and healthy relationships.

The Four Goals of Family Life: Jagannathesvari Devi Dasi

The Four Goals of Family Life is a comprehesive guide explaining the fourfold path of dharma, artha, kama, moksha (righteous action, economic development, sense gratification, and liberation), and describing how to balance and regulate the four pursuits for a happy married life. This is an excellent reference book for Grihastha life.

The Nurtured Heart Approach- Books by Howard Glasser

Howard has written several books based on his unique approach. Although Howard's books are geared mainly towards parents and teachers, the 'honey bee' principle of giving our energy to success is a powerful one and can be applied in any relationship context.

The Third Alternative - Stephen Covey

This Third Alternative concept is a wonderful and creative way of solving our problems by coming up with a solution that works for everyone.

Listening, The Forgotten Skill - Madelyn Burley-Allen

Just one example of the many good books that teach effective listening skills.

Men Are from Mars, Women Are from Venus: A Practical Guide for Improving Communication & Getting What You Want. - John Gray PhD

Classic book that helps us to understand the different communication styles between men and women and the psychology behind it.

Made in the USA
Middletown, DE
23 September 2021